To Dad (Otho E. Thomas), Granddads (Lilbourne Thomas and Lynn Boyd Bell), and Great Granddads (James Knox Thomas and W.J. Simmons) - Great story tellers all. If you are looking down at me and reading over my shoulder - enjoy. I miss all of you.

Bill R. Thomas

TABLE OF CONTENTS

Chapter   **Page**

Introduction A. - Character Stories   1

1   The Barking Dog Never Bites, Well - Almost Never   2

2   Monk Fetches The Doctor   10

3   The Shepherd of the Pennyrile   13

4   Praying for Rain   21

5   The Horse Race   26

6   Hatched on a Fence Post   30

Introduction B. - Animal Stories   32

7   The Most Valuable Horse That Ever Lived   34

8   Amos - The Grading Dog   48

9   Turpentine - A Good Dog Mover   50

10   The Bulldog and Monkey Fight   53

11   Ole Ripper   59

12   The Virile Rooster   67

13   Just Identifying Myself - That's All   73

14   Got The Dead Wood On You Now   76

15   Talking To The Animals   78

16   The Creamed Cat   85

17   The Blue Ribbon Cow   88

18   The First Consultant   91

Preface

I must be getting old; when I talk to my offspring about the good old days before T..V., iphones, etc. they look at me as if I were Methulusa. Then they say "Why Dad (or Papa Bear-Granddad), what did you do for entertainment in those good old days?" I then explained that we entertained one another by telling stories. They want me to illustrate and when I start a good story, the phone rings, the door bell chimes, or someone's favorite T.V. show comes on and they scatter long before I complete the story and get to the "punch line". In frustration then, I decided to write down some of these tales, as best I can remember them before old Al S. Heimer strikes and they are lost forever in my memory.

There are probably thousands of such tales that were told around the fireside, under a big shade trees, on the bench in front of the courthouse, etc. back before the days of television. Most of those stories were not only entertaining; they conveyed some of the lessons of life. I had the good fortune of growing up in rural West Kentucky with a Dad, a Granddad, and a Great Granddad (Who I well remember) that were each, in their own style, great storytellers.

This book is a collection of some of those stories which I remember from the good old days (definition-the "days of our youth"). I don't claim any credit of authorship for any of these tales. I suspect that you could go to most any good library and find tales similar to these-some better, some not. Perhaps the author was the originator of the tale - perhaps not. My Great Grandfather claimed that some of the tales he told originated back in the old country - Wales. All I can say is "I didn't copy these from any book".

In general, times were sort of tough, back in the good old days. However, folks helped one another out and they always maintained their inborn sense of humor. Unlike the stuff on TV today, these stories didn't contain a lot of sex and violence. They were mostly about folks and animals and everyday living.

The best (most entertaining) storytellers were those who had mastered the art of colorful language and the art of timing. my Granddad was a master of both. As I write some of these stories I can still hear him telling him.

I also figured that I had better get three stories written while folks can still read.

By Bill Thomas

P.S.
I've changed the names of most folks to protect the guilty.

Chapter		Page

Introduction C. - Politics, Religion, Medicine, and the Law		92
19	The Best Political Speech Ever Made	93
20	Faith vs. Knowledge	97
21	Firearm on my Hip	100
22	Little Black Pills	101
23	Some Prayers Are Answered	104
24	Free Medical Advice - Worth What It Costs	106
25	Seen Us	109
Introduction D. - Hunting Stories		110
26	Squirrel Hunting Scare	111
27	Bird Hunting During The Great War	116
28	Slingshot Charlie	123
29	Fox Hunting	126
30	Big Bad Bear	131
Introduction E. - Stories Close to Home		135
31	Good Bourbon And Bad Moonshine	136
32	Mind Your Table Manners	140
33	Maine	143
34	Can't Find My Fistes	145
35	Tobacco Crop Money	149
36	Chawin Tebaccer	167
37	Uncle Bob's Flying Machine	171
38	Spooks and Goblins	175
39	Uncle Dewey's Motor Sickle	183

Chapter		Page

Introduction F. - Sexy Stories		194
40	A Sure Bet	196
41	Fast Women	199
42	Thou Shalt Not	203
43	That's One	213
44	Fooled Her	217
45	Pinch and Judy	219
46	Beautiful Dreamer	223

A. CHARACTER STORIES

It has been, and always will be, that when you get a group of folks together there is going to be some "Characters". That's just the way we are built.

Stories about the most colorful of these characters are told and retold - generation after generation. The two characters in this class from my neck of the woods were Ernie Guy Hickerson and Monk Frankel. The Ernie Guy and Monk stories I remember are:

Chapter

1   The Barking Dog Never Bites; Well - Almost Never

2   Monk Fetches The Doctor

3   The Shepherd of the Pennyrile

4   Praying For Rain

5   The Horse Race

6   Hatched On A Fence Post

CHAPTER 1

THE BARKING DOG NEVER BITES; WELL - ALMOST NEVER

Ernie Guy Hickerson was known far and wide throughout West Kentucky, but particularly in Hopkins, Caldwell, and Christian counties, for his aversion to steady work and for his wit. He traveled around the country side, living off his wits primarily: although he would work a few hours now and then if there was a dry place to sleep and a hot meal waiting at the end of his labors.

He was fair hand working tobacco and haying and would even cut wood if pressed hard. The following are few stories I remember my Granddad and Dad told about Ernie Guy:

Ernie Guy was doing some work for my granddad (Lilbourne or just "Lib" to most) during the summer when the blackberries were ripening. My grandmother (Matilda or "Tildy" to most) was an excellent cook and didn't believe she had served an adequate meal unless she had several meats, vegetables, breads, and desserts on the table. Ernie Guy knew that and he always stopped at their farm whenever he was in that part of the country;

EXCELLENT SUFFICIENCY:

Ernie Guy had spent the morning in the field with Lib and when they came into the house for lunch, the table fare included Ernie Guy's favorite- fried chicken. When he came through the door and smelled it he said "UMMMM....FRIED CHICKUN!! They washed and sat down and Ernie snitched a piece while Lib was saying grace and cleared the platter as soon as amen was said. After he disposed of the chicken, Tildy tried to serve him some ham meat and beans but he declined and rared back and said "Thank you anyway Miz Tildy but I done had an excellent sufficiency"

Those at the table in addition to my grandparents and Ernie Guy were the five youngest of my aunts and uncles (it was a large family -14 children to be exact). Tildy got up and went to the stove and returned with a huge blackberry cobbler and sat it on the table and asked aunt Cora to serve and aunt Mildred to get a pitcher of cream to pour on it. Cora got bowls from the cupboard and served everyone cobbler - everyone except Ernie Guy. Tildy saw the kicked dog look on Ernie Guy's face and said "Cora, aren't you going to serve Ernest any pie?" She said "No Mama, he already had an excellent sufficiency" Ernie Guy sat up straight and stuttered and blustered before it finally came out "Why Miss Cora, everybody knows that excellent sufficiency means before Miz Tildy's blackberry cobbler".

They were visiting around the table after everyone had finished eating and uncle Stallard looked at Ernie Guy and asked "Ernie, do you think you will ever marry you a wife who will cook you fried chicken and cobbler?" Ernie thought for a minute and replied" Why shore - the good book says that for every goose there shall be a gander - I just ain't found mine yet".

These next Ernie Guy stories were told by my Dad:

THE HIGH AND THE MIGHTY:

One of the many dreaded tasks in raising tobacco was the hanging (racking) of the leaves in the tobacco barn so they would cure properly before the tobacco was sold. The tobacco stalks were cut and attached to a tobacco stick. Each stick would contain maybe twelve stalks (plants). This was done in the field as the tobacco was harvested and they generally were loaded onto a sled or wagon and hauled to the tobacco barn where a group of men would rack them on the cross members for that purpose. The barns were pyramid shaped so the man who worked at the top of the pyramid shape handled every stick but the men who worked at the bottom of the pyramid handled only every other or every third stick.

Once during tobacco harvest, Ernie guys stopped at Lib's place the night before they were going to rack tobacco. Before Ernie was fed supper he "volunteered" to help with the tobacco the next day. After supper the conversation was maneuvered around to talking about the mighty kings in the olden days - King Herod, King Soloman, etc. - and how the highest were the mightiest and vice versa. (There was a purpose for this subject - someone was getting set up to take the highest spot on the racking crew tomorrow (of course - Ernie).

The next morning when they got to the barn, Lib asked "Who is going to be the high and mighty King today. Everyone looked at Ernie and he said "Mr. Lib, I been a slave all my life and just don't rightly know how to be a king; I think Otho would make a fine king though. And that's how dad became king for a day.

VICIOUS DOGS

Not everyone welcomed Ernie Guy as my grandparents did. In fact, some of the folks around the country just plain didn't want him stopping at their place for one reason or another. (I neglected to explain earlier that Ernie didn't bathe regularly and never shaved and he had a certain wild look about him, although he was harmless.)

The Smith family whose farm jointed granddad's place on the west were one such family who just didn't want Ernie Guy around them - yet he always stopped at their farm when he came through. Ernie claimed the Smith place had the sweetest water and grew the best watermelons he ever tasted (apparently he thought there was a connection). One day Mr. Smith asked granddad if he knew of anything that would keep Ernie Guy off a fellers property? Granddad said

"I'm sure he wouldn't want to get dog bit – so I guess a couple of vicious dogs might do the trick." Mr. Smith agreed.

Smith put out the word around the country that he was in the market for a couple of the meanest, orneriest, most vicious hound dogs available. Granddad, being an old horse trader decided he would help his neighbor and make a dollar or two in the process, so he went to Princeton the next first Monday and shopped around for some mean dogs. Sure enough, he came across a feller who had a couple of Plott hounds which he had traded for down in Tennessee – claimed they were bear dogs. Pa Thomas traded for the two bear dogs and headed home with them tied in the bed of the wagon.

When he got home he turned the dogs loose and they promptly lit into his fox hounds and whipped them as well as a couple of bird dogs that belonged to Stallard. Soon, all the dogs on the places were hiding under the house and all the cats had climbed trees. Pa Thomas thought, I've got the perfect dogs for Mr. Smith. He sent Calvin to fetch Mr. Smith.

When Smith arrived and saw what had happened to the Thomas' dogs and cats and got a good look at the two brindle colored "bear dogs" he asked" How much will you take for them Lib?" Pa Thomas quoted a ridiculous price and they commenced to horse trade. Smith left leading the Plott hounds and he was happy. Pa Thomas figured he made a 1% profit and he was happy. (Granddad figured if you bought something for $1 and sold it for $2 – your profit was 1%).

Somehow, word traveled faster in those days than it does today and the word was that Ernie Guy was about a mile east of the Thomas farm and headed west. Again, Calvin was sent to the Smith place to warn them. He did and came back and waited at the front gate for Ernie. In a few minutes Ernie wandered up and Calvin told him that the Smiths had something for him. He passed up the Thomas place and went directly to the Smith's.

The Smith's house was up on a hill, about 250 yards from the dirt road. Ernie always sang as he walked or trotted down the road and everyone could hear him for a half mile or so. He had a deep gruff voice. He turned off the road and headed up the hill toward the Smith house.

Smith kept the Plott hounds in the corn crib and when he heard Ernie coming he slipped out to the corn crib and let the hounds loose with a sharp "Sic Em". The hounds heard Ernie and took out after him, barking and baying as they went, hackles raised. Smith ran around the house and joined Mrs. Smith on their front porch to watch the show. According to Mrs. Smith, them vicious dawgs ran right at Ernie Guy just like they was a gonna eat him up. But when they got to about 50 feet from Ernie, he dropped down on all fours and commenced to GROWL in his deep bass voice and he charged straight at them vicious dogs. Well sir, them dogs didn't know what they was facing so they skidded to a halt but ole Ernie just kept becoming at them, growling all the way. Them vicious dogs finally tucked tail and run off in the woods as fast as they could run and Ernie chased them a ways. Far as we know they run all the way back to Tennessee.

Ernie saw the Smiths standing on the porch and he got up, brushed himself off and walked up to them. Ernie asked "Wonder where them wolves come from?" Smith said "Tennessee probably – come on in Ernie and wash up, we're about to eat dinner". Ernie said "Thank ye kindly, mind my asking what are we having?" "Crow" replied Smith.

CHAPTER 2

MONK FETCHES THE DOCTOR

Monk Frankel was known far and wide as the biggest liar in West Kentucky. He could tell some whoppers and most of them were so entertaining that folks would stop him and start a conversation just to hear some of his tall tales. The older Monk became, the bigger his lies became. The uninitiated would stand in awe and listen to him and sometimes the initiated fell for some of his tales. It was said that he could convince a newcomer that Calvin Cooledge, the then President, was going to preside at the next Masonic lodge meeting in Dawson. (He told that story several times and each time, a crowd gathered for the lodge meeting).

Jim Orange took great delight at picking at anyone, but especially Monk. But Jim's idea of fun sometimes bordered on intimidation and much uncomfort for the pickee. Jim was a big man and could be very ornery and obnoxious when he wanted to be. However, Jim was all right otherwise and everybody in the country thought a lot of his big fat wife, Hazel.

The Orange's lived about two miles out of Dawson, on the Cadiz Hill road, and Monk lived about two miles further west of them. The Fitts farm was about half way between them. One day Bud Hale and Monk were walking to Dawson and were coming up to the Orange Place. Monk spotted Jim Orange standing on his porch and he knew that he was in for trouble of some kind. Jim would try to make a fool out of him in front of Bud.

Monk wasn't a fool, however. He said to Bud "Lets walk purty fast past the Orange place; I don't want to be bothered by Big Jim this morning." So they speeded up. Sure enough, as they came a beam of the house, Jim yelled out "Hey Monk, stop for a minute and tell me one of your big lies."

Monk kept walking fast and yelled back "Sorry Mr. Jim, can't stop – Miz. Hazel fell out of a peach tree at the Fitts' place and broke her arm – me and Bud are going to Dawson now to fetch Doc Young."

Jim came unraveled at the news that his wife was hurt and he raised up out of the chair and started running up the road to the Fitts' place some mile distant. By the time he reached the Fitts' place, he was red in the face and huffing and puffing for air and could barely talk. Mrs. Fitts rushed out to meet him and exclaimed "Jim, what on earth is the matter?" Jim said "Hazel fell out of your peach tree and broke her arm". Mrs. Fitts asked "When?; I haven't seen Hazel since church last Sunday". Jim said" It must have happened just a few minutes ago, Monk Frankel came running past the house………..

Then he remembered – Hazel was in the house cooking dinner when Monk came by. He had been had – Monk did tell him another big lie.

CHAPTER 3

THE SHEPERD OF THE PENNYRILE

Cordy Crofton's farm was about the roughest and brushiest place in the country. It was hilly and the old land was poor and wouldn't grow much except weeds, scrub timber, and bramble briars. A few years ago Cordy had sold off the timber and quit trying to farm, he just raised a few head of livestock. He was a real tightwad and still had the first nickel he ever made so financially, he wasn't hurting.

It bothered Cordy that he wasn't making hardly anything off the farm cause there just wasn't enough good pasture for the few cows he ran. He was talking to Mr. Staples, a farmer from Christian county, who he had known for years, and Staples told him that he would be better off raising goats cause they would eat purt near anything – including weeds, leaves, and briars.

Cordy shopped around and finally found some goats at a bargain price. He bought ten nanny goats and one bill goat and turned them loose on his place. Sure enough, in a couple of years he had goats all over his place. The old billy goat must have put in some overtime. Cordy was right proud of himself - and of Billy too.

However, he had neglected to find out how to convert the goats to money. And he remembered he had paid forty dollars in hard cash money for these animals. To further complicate matters, he was starting to find the skeletons of dead goats in the woods and knew the bobcats and wild dogs were starting to feed on his herd. One morning he saddled his riding horse and rode to Mr. Staples place for advice. Staples told him "Heck, I didn't say you could ever convert them to money – I just told you they would eat weeds and briars". Cordy got on his horse and rode home, mad as a hornet at Staples.

But Cordy wasn't whipped yet. He considered himself one of the smartest men in the county; he could read and write – and he had plenty of times to figure things out. So he started going to the depot at Dawson just about every day, figuring that sooner or later he would bump into a train passenger that would know where and how he could sell them blamed goats. Now and then one of the passengers would leave a Louisville Courier Journal newspaper lying and Cordy would grab it and take it home with him and read it – word by word. It was during one of these newspaper reading sessions that the solution (or possible solution) jumped out of the printed page at him.

He read that the Baptists were going to have a big convention in Louisville in a few days and during the convention they would have a big barbecue. The next day he went to the New Century hotel in Dawson and "borrowed" some writing paper and an envelope. He wrote a letter to the Baptist Convention and offered to sell them to the meat they would need for their big barbecue at a real bargain price. He quoted $5 a head for grown goats and $2 a head for young goats. He hurried to the post office and mailed the letter.

Sure enough, in a few days Cordy received a letter back from the Baptist Convention – and they accepted his offer. The letter said one of their representatives would contact him on the eleventh to make arrangements for delivery and payment. The letter went on to say the representative would probably have a cattle car on the siding at Dawson and he would buy at least fifty head.

Cordy was elated. He read and reread the letter and each time he read it he would stop and figure out how much he was going to make on this goat deal. Each time he came out with $210. (50 x 5 = 250 – 40 = 210 clear profit). He was happy as a possum eating wild grapes and already started bragging to anyone who would listen about his big goat deal.

The next day Cordy stopped by Hamby's Well and stated bragging some more on his goat deal to Ollie Fields, one of the regular loafers. Ollie said "Cordy, Ain't you counting your chickens before they hatch?" "Heck no" angrily responded Cordy, "look at this letter" He showed the letter to Ollie said "I wasn't doubting you had a chance to sell them darn goats – I'm doubting you can catch them and get them to Dawson and loaded by the 11th – today is the 9th." Cordy said "I'll handle that when the man shows up." He left the crowd of loafers who were starting to hoorah him and went straight to the New Century hotel to see if the Baptist representative had arrived. He had. Cordy went to his room and talked to him and agreed to deliver 52 head of goats to the rail car on or before 9am the day after tomorrow.

Cordy was so excited he almost stopped at Woodburn's drug store to buy a coke and celebrate – almost. But he regained his senses before he wasted a nickel and started to figure how to solve his "delivery" problem. While he was standing in the shade and his money making brain was whirring, Butch Rambo walked up and spoke. They talked a while and Cordy finally told Butch about his problem. Butch said "If it was me I'd hire that Newsome boy to round them up horseback – they say he is a purty good cowboy" Cordy said, "I've already thought of that – won't work – too rough for a horse and them goats have gotten as wild as guineas since the wild dogs and bobcats has started killing them – it will take a fast man on foot to round them up" Butch interrupted, "Ole Monk could do it" So, Cordy headed straight to Monk's shack out west of Dawson.

Monk was sitting on a stump out front of his shack, puffing on his corn cob pipe, when Cordy rode up on his horse. Cordy dismounted and they said their "Howdies" then Cordy got right to the point. He told Monk that he wanted all the goats on his place rounded up and driven to the depot in Dawson by tomorrow night and he wanted to hire Monk to do the job. Monk asked "Why don't you just throw out some feed and let them round their own self's up?" Cordy lied that he didn't have any feed. Next, Monk asked "Why don't you

- 14 -

cowboy them up with that horse you are riding?" Again Cordy lied that he had something else he had to do.

Monk took a long drag on his pipe and said he would study on it – and asked "How much you willing to pay?" Cordy's brain went whirring again and he knew that old Monk didn't care about money and he didn't want to spend any of that $250 so he finally said. "Monk, tell you the truth, I don't really know how many goats is on my place but I'm sure there is a bunch of them. I contracted to sell most of the grown ones that we can deliver to the depot tomorrow. Here is what I'm willing to do – I'll keep all the grown stuff you can round up and I'll give you half of all the young stuff you bringin. Does that sound fair enough?"

Monk puffed on his pipe a minute and asked "Does that mean you will decide which half I get?" Cordy thought and said "No, this is what we'll do – I pick one and you pick one and so on. Monk asked "What if there is an extra one?" Cordy knew he had him now, so he said "If there is an extra - he's yours." Monk said "Aye gawd, you got a deal, let's get started." Cordy said,. "Let's wait till tomorrow – see you about sunup" and he mounted his riding horse and rode off.

True to his word, ole Monk showed up at Cordy's place right a daybreak. Cordy invited him in and fed him some ham and eggs. They got up from the table and went outside. Monk shuffled his feet and started to say something a couple of times, but didn't. Cordy noticed and said "What's troubling you Monk?" Monk replied" Well sir, I'm ready to start herding in them goats for you but I can't remember for sure just zackly what them critters look like" Cordy said "Don't feel bad about that Monk; they look sort of like a deer and go baa, baa. But all I got on the place now is them goats so you might as well round up everything you come across, that is if you can. I realize you are getting old and some of them goats is very fast and if you can't herd them all in, that's all right" He added., "I'll leave the gate to the barnyard open and you can gather them up there and I'll help you drive the bunch to the rail car at the depot" Monk was stung by the reference to him getting old and slow and he said as he broke off a small limb to switch himself". Ay gawd, I'll be back before lunch with every darn goat on this place." With that said, Monk whacked himself on the leg with the switched yelled "Git up Blue, we got work to do" and he took off. (Monk always pretended he was riding a horse which he called Blue.)

Cordy went out to the barn and opened the gate to the barnyard as he had promised. He could hear Monk swatting himself and yelling as he crashed through the brush on his roundup. He decided to climb up to the hay loft to see what he could see of the roundup; and now and again he got a glimpse of goats running with Monk right on their heels, yelling and whipping Blue. He finally got out of sight so Cordy went back to the house to have more coffee. In about 45 minutes he heard Monk yelling "Open the gate, I'm coming in with the first gather." Cordy jumped up and ran to the gate and got there about the time Monk topped the hill with the darndest menagerie of critters out in front of him that you ever saw. He expertly herded them through the gate into the barnyard and Cordy closed the gate. Monk didn't even slow down and headed back out and yelled over his shoulder "Be back directly with the rest of our herd."

Cordy decided he would just have a smoke and wait for him and try to keep this first catch penned. His sheep dog had come out of the barn and was doing a good job of that already, but he thought he might be needed before Monk got back. He guessed that Monk had brought in close to fifty on his first pass, and Cordy thought he saw a couple in the bunch that looked like deer.

In about 30 minutes Cordy heard Monk coming back toward the barn – switching his britches leg and yelling "Come on Blue". When Cordy saw Monk top the hill and head for the barn, he opened the gate and got the sheep dog out of the pen to help corral the new gather that Monk was herding in. When all the critters were inside he closed the gate and Monk rode up and said "Mr. Cordy, if you don't mind I'm goin to stop a minute and get me a drink of water and rest a little. They walked up to the house and Monk got his drink and they went out on the porch and sat for a while. Cordy asked "how much you got left?" And Monk said he had covered the entire place but there was a few young ones back in the far corner that got away on his last pass and he was going back to get them. Cordy said "Aw heck, if that's all there is left just leave them". Monk said "Ain't you forgettin something?" Cordy asked "What?" Monk snorted "Half of them is mine".

With that point cleared, Monk jumped up and took off. He was gone nearly an hour on this pass but finally returned with a whole bunch of little stuff. They got them penned finally and Cordy got a piece of brown paper sack and a stubby pencil and they took inventory. When he had finished this is what he had written down:

```
Goats:
   Billies            21
   Nannies            86
   Kids               55
Deer:
   Bucks               8
   Does               23
   Fawns              14
Rabbits               27
            Total    234
```

Cordy showed the list to Monk and said your share comes to 38 head. Monk couldn't read so he asked Cordy to read what the paper said to him and Cordy did. Monk said "Darn if I don't believe them young rabbit goats weren't the hardest ones of the bunch to herd in".

CHAPTER 4

PRAYING FOR RAIN

Ace McGregor told about one spring when he "contracted" with Ernie Guy to help him plant tobacco. In those days "settin out tobacco" was a back wrenching job and no one liked it. It was done by hand. (Today of course it is done by machine). After the ground was plowed and made ready and the rows laid by, you took a bucket of tobacco plants and a peg (sharpened stick) and went down the row punched a hole in the rows every 2 feet and placed a tobacco plant in it and covered the roots by hand. They were usually long rows so that by the time you got to the end of a row your body was C shaped and you couldn't straighten up to a I shape so you just sort of spun around and crossed to the next row and started back. Ernie had planted tobacco before and he knew how hard the work was. The only way that Ace had been able to contract him was to offer a silver dollar a day plus keep and promise they would have friend chicken every day. (The going rate was 50 cents a day).

Ernie Guy showed up at the McGregor place on the second day of April. It had not rained in weeks and the ground was powder dry. Hardly any grass had greened up, the spring flowers hadn't bloomed, and even the weeds were stunted. It was fast becoming a very serious drought.

Ace told Ernie that they couldn't start setting tobacco until it came a good soaking rain. Ernie sort of shuffled his feet and stewed around a bit and finally said "Mr. Ace, I ain't got no other work lined up and no place to go nor no food to eat". Ace said "Heck fire Ernie, I didn't ask you to leave – there's lots of stuff that needs to be done around here and you can just stay here and help me till we get a good rain." He added "It always rains in April and I've been seeing clouds build in the west every day, all we need to do is pray for rain" Ernie said "You are right Mr. Ace, I'll stay. What do you want me to do?"

Ace knew that Ernie was a good "handyman" and could do most anything around the farm so he outlined the following projects for him:

1. Check all the horses good and shoe any that need shoeing.
2. Check all the harness good, oil it, and patch any that needs it.
3. Ride all the fences and patch any that needs it.
4. Gather all the cows and calves, dehorn any that needs it, castrate the bull calves, and notch the left ear of the Jersey bull (look at a cow's ear to see what kind of notch to make).
5. Clean out the chicken house and scatter the manure on the garden.
6. Chop some stove wood for the Misses.
7. Harness up a team and hook up the bucket and clean out the pond in the west pasture and take a chopping ax and chop up the willow tree that blew down and is laying in the pond.

Ace said "That ought to be enough to get you started – if it don't rain before you finish, I'll think of more stuff to do."

Ernie Guy immediately went to work and Ace would check up on him now and then – not to see if he was working (he knew Ernie worked) – but to see if he needed any help.

The morning of April 7th it got real cloudy and thundered a time or two while they were eating breakfast. Ace noticed that Ernie was sort of depressed. Ernie finished his bacon and eggs and said he would hitch up; the team and start work on the pond and try to get it finished before it started to rain. Ace said "OK".

By mid morning it was still threatening rain, though not a drop had fallen. Ace decided he would walk back to the west pasture and see how Ernie was doing. When he came in view of the pond, he saw the team hitched to a bush but he couldn't see Ernie. He became concerned and rushed toward the pond and before he walked up to the team he could hear Ernie's deep voice but he could not see him. He walked on up to the pond and listened. It sounded like Ernie was praying and that he was over behind the dam. He took a few steps toward the dam and listened again and heard the following:

"Lord, I ain't askin you to blow them rain clouds away. We need the rain – everybody knows how bad we need a little shower. What I'm askin Lord is for you to give us enough rain to make the grass grow so the livestock will have plenty to eat, and enough to make the spring flowers grow so the women folk will be happy, and enough to fill the ponds and creeks so the fish and frogs and water creatures will prosper, and maybe enough to melt the chicken manure that I scattered on the garden so I can plant the garden. But Lord, please Lord, whatever you do, don't give us a good soaker so we'll have to start setting tobacco."   AMEN

CHAPTER 5

THE HORSE RACE

Monk Frankel always traveled the dirt roads around the country side a foot –
except he pretended he was riding his horse named "Blue". He would never
accept a ride in a wagon or buggy, even if it was offered. Monk always claimed
he could get wherever he was going quicker on old Blue – he always traveled at a
trot or all out run – he never just walked.

Old doctor Boitnett (Doc) served the entire county and traveled by buggy. He
always kept the best and fastest pair of horses around and took great pride in
them. One of his greatest pleasures was bragging on his horses. Now and then
he would come up on Monk and he always stopped and chatted (Monk knew all
the gossip). Likewise, he always offered Monk a ride in his fast buggy, but
Monk always declined and would trot along behind the buggy.

Doc stopped at Orange's store one day and visited the "Whittle and Spit"
crowd while he ate some cheese and crackers and drank an RC cola. The group
was discussing Monk – especially how fast he could run. Doc took the
opportunity to brag on his buggy horses so he interrupted and said "I take
exception to your assessment of Monk's speed – especially about him being able
to outrun a horse. I come across Monk out on the roads every now and again and

I always pass him and leave him eating dust". No one argued with old Doc and it got real quiet in the store and Doc left.

It was less than a week later when Doc was driving down the Piney Grove road toward Dawson. He had just delivered a baby at the McIntosh place and was feeling right proud of himself (newborns always affected him in that way). He saw someone trotting in the road up ahead, also going toward Dawson, and as he drew closer he could tell that it was Monk. He put the whip to the horses and soon caught up with him and stopped for the usual visit. Monk was not very talkative and, in fact, was not friendly. Doc cut the visit short and asked "Where you heading Monk?" "Dawson" was Monk's reply. "Hop in and I'll give you a ride" offered Doc.

Monk spat back "No thanks, I'm in a hurry. Got to get there before the stores close." TWACK! TWACK! Monk hit his britches leg with his switch and said "Git moving Blue". He was in full stride after a couple of steps and left Doc and his prancing pair of buggy horses in his dust.

Doc sat there for a second and soon figured out what had happened – someone had told Monk what he had said at Oranges' store the other day and Monk had just challenged him to a race. By darn, he thought, if it is a race he wants, I'll give it to him. He reached over and got the buggy whip, got a good hold of the reins, and started whipping the team and yelling encouragement to them as they set out after old Monk and Blue. Despite the lashing by both the whip and the tongue, the best Doc was able to do was to just get Monk in sight for a brief moment. After about a five mile race, Dawson soon came into view and Monk was actually pulling away from Doc and his fast horses. Monk started hollering when he got to town and ran clear across town. Doc stopped at his office. It was obvious to any onlookers what had taken place.

The horse race soon became the main subject of the local gossip and kids would snicker and point at Doc's horses whenever he drove by. Doc couldn't stand it and disappeared for several days. His disappearance was added to the gossip until Milt Stone came forward and said he saw Doc buy a train ticket for Lexington – and even saw him board the train. This information was confirmed when Doc returned with a thoroughbred race horse he had made the trip to purchase.

About three months later there was a rumor out of Princeton about this little man come racing through town switching his legs closely followed by an old grey headed man in a buggy being pulled by a thoroughbred racing horse. This story was ever confirmed; nor was it denied by old Doc Boitnett who, incidentally, was the first person in the county to buy one of them new fangled motor cars.

CHAPTER 6

HATCHED ON A FENCE POST

Monk finished chopping a big stack of stove wood for the widow, Mrs. Wilson, and she fed him a big lunch consisting of fried country ham, mashed potatoes, green beans, squash, biscuits, gravy, and milk. She also paid him fifty cents – cash money.

Monk headed down the road toward Crossroads (where Orange's store was located). Although his belly was full, his sweet tooth was giving him a strong signal. He was making good time, occasionally switching his britches leg and say "Get along now Blue", but the closer he got to the store the stronger the urge to get something sweet became. When he got to the store he pulled up and went inside and spent a whole dime of his hard earned money for an RC cola and a moon pie. He took them outside and joined the "Spit and Whittle Club" that was congregated under a big sycamore tree.

The subject of the day was "ancestors, places of birth, family trees, and relatives".

Billy Bob Lukus asked Monk "Where was you born Monk?" Monk replied "Wasn't borned – a big bird (presumed by all to mean a stork but Monk probably meant a buzzard) swooped down out of the sky, landed on a fence post and laid a egg. The hot sun hatched that egg and that was me."

B. ANIMAL STORIES

In the early Kentucky rural areas, perhaps the most important thing to the country folk were the animals, both domestic and wild. There were encounters between people and animals every day. At sunrise they got up and milked the cows, fed the chickens and horses, and slopped the hogs – usually before they ate breakfast. Every barn had a few cats around it to control the rodents and every yard contained a couple of hounds for hunting and a little feist dog for the women folk and kids. And the woods were full of wild things. It is only natural then that many of the tales passed on from generation to generation were about animals. The following are a few that I remember:

Chapter

7 The Most Valuable Horse That Ever Lived

8 Amos – The Grading Dog

9 Turpentine – A Good Dog Mover

10 The Bulldog and Monkey Fight

11 Ole Ripper

12 The Virile Rooster

13 Just Identifying Myself – That's All

14 Got the Dead Wood on You Now

15 Talking to the Animals

16 The Creamed Cat

17 The Blue Ribbon Cow

18 The First Consultant

CHAPTER 7

THE MOST VALUABLE HORSE THAT EVER LIVED

Kentucky has long been famous for its fine tobacco, smooth bourbon whiskey, beautiful horses, and fast women. For those of you unfamiliar with Kentucky geography, etc., the whiskey is distilled in the central part of the state (Louisville, Elizabethtown, Bardstown areas), and tobacco is grown throughout the state. The most beautiful horses are raised in the bluegrass area (Lexington) and the Kentucky women are fast enough to cover the entire state. The reason I'm telling you this is because it was highly unusual that the most valuable horse that ever lived was in west Kentucky, which ain't famous for anything particularly.

There is a long story behind this invaluable animal (name of Bituminous) but I'll cut it short and try to cover the highlights.

Sam Parker had taken a load of burley tobacco to Hoptown (Hopkinsville) to sell and he got a right good price for it. After he visited a bar or two and kicked up his heels a little, he decided to head back to his place just outside of Dawson. He climbed into his old Ford stake bed truck and pulled out of Hoptown about dark. Old Sam wasn't drunk, but he wasn't exactly sober either – just in that mellow in between zone. It being dusk and Sam being mellow, it wouldn't have been safe to meet him on the road or to try to cross the road in front of him either. He hadn't gone but four or five miles down the narrow and curvy road when

Fazil Johnson tried to do just that – he was leading his mare across the road from the pasture to the barnyard just at the time that Sam was coming around the curve. Sam saw them, but too late. He hit the brakes and started skidding and sliding. Fazil had the presence of mind to turn loose of the bridle and dive into the bar ditch. Sam missed Fazil but made glue factory ammunition out of the old black mare and tore up the front end of this old truck.

Sam got out of the truck to survey the damage and Fazil climbed out of the bar ditch and started cussing Sam, threatening him with a law suit, bodily harm, and various other things too terrible to mention.

Sam was feeling no pain and didn't pay too much attention to Fazil's threats. However, he did catch one thing that Fazil said and that was that the old mare had a little bitty black colt that would starve to death and would be added to Sam's crimes (He had already found Sam guilty of murder) Sam had a soft spot for animals, particularly baby animals, and he figured he was going to have to pay Fazil $40 or $50 dollars for the old mare to shut him up ; so he may as well try to salvage something out of the deal. He asked "Where is the little colt?" Fazil; replied "Over in the barn". Sam said " Mind if I take a look at him?" Fazil said " Naw, but we'll walk over there - I'm afraid if you drive that durned truck, you'll run into my barn and destroy it too". They walked to the barn, went inside and Fazil led the way to the stall where the colt was. When they stepped into the stall, the colt was lying down but got up and stood on wobbly legs to greet them. The colt was jet black, like its mother, and Sam commented that he was as black as #9 bituminous coal (which was mined locally).

Sam asked " How much you take for this scrawny, half starved, ugly looking little ole colt?" Fazil replied" We ain't settled on how much you pay for that fine registered thoroughbred mare who was this colt's mammy before you went and murdered her". Sam said "Aw heck, I figured we would call that even" Fazil asked" What the heck you mean - call it even?". Sam said" I would not charge you for fixin up my truck which your old black bag of bones tore up providing you didn't charge me for that old buzzard bait". Fazil said" You're crazy as a bessy bug, you run over that horse and killed it". Sam said "I had the right of way and you was breakin the law". Fazel exclaimed "Breakin the law?!!!". You're crazy as a loon". Sam said "I may be, but I know it is again the law to lead a black horse across the road after dark unless you're carrying a lantern or some kind of light - and if you don't believe me we'll hop in my truck and drive to Judge Parker's place and prove it. And, by the way, the judge just happens to be my second cousin."

This turn of events set Fazil to thinking so he said "Tell you what I'll do, I'll take $200 for the both of them, mare and foal." Sam said" I was thinking more like $50 for the colt only". Fazil said "I had best call my first cousin, Sheriff Jim Ned Johnson, and get his opinion on this deal before I make a big mistake". It didn't take Sam long to change his counter offer to $100 and Fazil accepted. Sam pulled out his poke which had the $300 he had left from the tobacco sale, and peeled off five twenty dollar bills, Sam gathered up the colt in his arms and placed him in the cab of his old Ford truck, got in, and headed for his farm.

Well sir, when he got home with the unweaned orphan colt, there was such commotion made by his wife and kids that it was days before Mrs. Parker noticed the battered front end of his truck or realized that a part of the tobacco crop money was missing. They found an old baby bottle and everyone took turns "nursing" the orphan colt. He became a part of the Parker family in short order. The kids called him Mackie, Mrs. Parker called him Midnight, but Sam continued to call him Bituminous and that name finally prevailed.

Time passed and Bituminous grew and grew. He turned out to be a right nice jet black horse, but he wasn't good for anything except a pet. They never bothered to break him to ride or to harness, but when anyone went into the field with him he would immediately trot over and want to be petted. He was very lovable.

More time passed and the children grew up and one by one left home until there was only Sam and the misses left - plus Bituminous of course. With the passage of time, things changed around Dawson. The state had bought up some of the sorry old land around Dawson and built a nice lake and opened a state park that began to attract tourist - especially during the summer. Some of the tourist must have liked it around Dawson for several retired folks moved there.

One of the new arrivals was the Schwartz family, Lester and Jean. Sam sold them two acres out of his front pasture and they built a little two bedroom house on it and moved in. Sam and Lester got to be purty good buddies They both had a taste for good bourbon. Each kept a supply on hand and they would get together most every day and sip a little bourbon. Sam loved the stories that Lester told about living in Chicago and Lester loved to hear Sam's tales about growing up around Dawson. Lester also liked Sam's horse and got to feeding him apples through the fence. Sam didn't like that much but he never said anything about it.

One night when Lester came over to Sam's and they had a snort or two, Lester started telling a wild tale about the time he chased a couple of thugs from the John Dillinger gang out of his furniture store in Chicago - using only a broom. Sam thought, now's the time - so he tried to borrow some money from Lester while Lester was puffed up and feeling proud of himself. But Lester let on like he didn't hear him and changed the subject and went right on talking.

Sam interrupted the next story and hit him up for a loan again. Lester couldn't ignore the issue any further so he asked "How much you need?" Lester explained he had to have $30 immediately to pay the dentist so he could get his store bought teeth. Lester studied for a minute and finally said "Samuel, I'll tell you what I'm gonna do – I'm going to buy that old black horse from you for $50". Sam replied "Oh no, I could never sell Bituminous, he's just like one of the family". There was complete silence and Sam finally realized that Lester wasn't going to loan him a dime, much less $30. Reality can be brutal thing, and reality had just hit Sam in the pocket book so he finally said, just barely above a whisper, "Lester, if you promise to take real good care of old Bituminous, and give me a chance to him back when I get on my feet again, I'll let you have him for $100". Lester turned his back to Sam and said "Maybe $60" Sam said "$90 is my bottom offer" Lester said "$75 is my top offer" and Sam said "Sold".

Who knows what possessed Lester to buy that old horse. Maybe it was because the old horse would come up to the fence and whiney for him to come out and pet him or maybe even to bring him an apple or lump of sugar – and Lester didn't have many friends, especially after Jean passed away. Or maybe he just wanted to help Sam, who had also been a friend to him, and was opposed to loaning money in general and to friends in particular. Whatever the reason, Sam was going to get his new teeth and Lester now owned a horse.

Sam didn't sleep well that night. All he could think about was his departed pet, and his wife had not been very understanding when he told her about selling old Bituminous. Early the next morning Sam was knocking on Lester's door – he wanted to swap back, teeth or no teeth. Lester wouldn't hear of it, he said "A deal is a deal". A bitter argument ensued and it ended when Lester said he wouldn't sell Bituminous under any circumstances – except maybe for $150 cash money. Sam left determined to hustle up the money some way so he could buy old Bituminous back from the old tightwad.

Sam spent the next few days trying to figure out how he could come up with some money and Lester spent the next few days getting better acquainted with (and more attached) to old Bituminous. Finally Sam hit upon a bright idea. The old lady had accumulated several quilts which she had sewed over the years; he decided he would sneak a few of them out of the closet and sell them to the tourist who visited the state park. He had seen peddlers at the park entrance selling chalk statues, felt pictures, and chenille bedspreads. If tourist would buy that stuff, most certainly they would buy genuine handmade quilts. Yep, he would go into the quilt business.

He snuck around and made some signs, Home Made Quilts - $10 each. He hid the signs in his truck. On Saturday morning when the Misses went to gather the eggs, Sam snuck some quilts out of the closet and hid them in his truck, also. After messing around the house a while, he finally told his wife he had to go to Dawson to get his new teeth. She wanted to go along but he convinced her otherwise and drove off and headed straight for the park entrance and as soon as he got there he parked in the spot he had seen the other peddlers use and immediately set up shop. He stretched a rope between two trees and hung the quilts on it and leaned his signs up against his truck. He filled his pipe with tobacco, lit it, and sat on the running board of his old Ford pick up to wait for the customers.

Business was sort of slow since the tourist season was not yet in full swing and he only sold three quilts before he decide he had better get on back home. He had a devil of a time explaining why he didn't return with his new teeth but she finally dropped the subject. Sunday morning he convinced her he was going fishing with Buck Smith and would back before dark. He headed back to the park entrance and again set up shop. He was more relaxed today since he didn't have to leave before dark. Maybe his relaxed attitude helped him sell; something did, for by mid afternoon he had sold out. He thought about returning to the house and trying to gather up some more inventory but the thought of the consequences if he got caught and put that thought out of his mind. Instead, he counted his money. What a pleasant surprise, he had $120 cash. He still had the $75 at home in a fruit jar also. It was time to visit Lester. He rushed home and dug $30 out of the jar and headed straight to Lester's. He pounded on Lester's back door and when Lester opened it, Sam thrust the $150 in his hand. At first, Lester tried to refuse the money but when he saw Sam's toothless smile turn in to a threatening scowl, he shoved the money in his pocket and went to get the bridle. In moments, Sam was leading old Bituminous back to his place.

A few weeks passed and the experience of the "horse trade' had put a damper on the friendship between Sam and Lester. Lester, who was now a widower, began to get mighty lonesome and longed for Sam's companionship and for the friendly whiney and nudges of old Bituminous. Sam had put the horse in a back pasture so Lester couldn't even see him. Lester couldn't stand it any longer so he went over to Sam's place and said he wanted to buy old Bituminous back.

At first Sam said "Heck No", but he started to soften up a little when he saw the hurt in poor ole Sam's eyes. Finally Sam said "Lester old buddy, I'll sell that horse to you for $500, providing I can come over to your place and see him any time I feel like it". Lester said "You got a deal". Lester said, "If you will put the bridle on him and follow me back to my place, I'll give you a check". Lester was about to back out of the deal, he didn't trust personal checks, but he remembered hearing in the barber shop that Lester was one of the biggest depositors in the Commercial Bank of Dawson, so he decided his check would probably be ok.

They led the horse over to Lester's and Sam got his check. It was Sunday and he would take it to the bank in the morning to get it cashed. The next morning, Sam was at the bank when it opened and there was no problem cashing the check. He took the money home and put it in his bank "fruit jar".

The next morning Sam decided he would go over to Lester's and check on old Bituminous. Lester wasn't friendly at all and refused to let him go out to his shed and see the horse. Sam left in a huff and vowed to get even with that welcher.

Sam laid awake most of the night trying to figure out how he could get even. He really could not come up with anything satisfactory. He finally decided the best he could do was buy the horse back and not let Lester see him again. But coming up with a price was a problem, and coming up with the money was even a greater problem. Wait a minute, he could write a check. The next morning, Sam headed to the bank and opened up a bank account. He deposited $250 and they gave him some temporary checks and said his personalized checks would be ready in a week. Sam waited for the personalized checks to arrive before he approached Lester again.

He knocked on Lester's back door and Lester invited him in for a cup of coffee. He was friendly again for some unknown reason. They talked a while before Sam finally said "I want to buy old Bituminous back". Lester said "OK, I'll sell him for $5000". Sam nodded and reached for his checkbook and wrote out a check for the purchase price and handed it to Lester. Lester reluctantly took the check and asked "Is this check any good?" Sam said " You sorry doubter, I took your check didn't I?" Sam left leading the old black horse who was moving mighty slow.

Later that afternoon, Lester was knocking on Sam's door. Sam invited him in and served some good bourbon. The conversation soon got around to old Bituminous and before he gave it much thought Lester had offered $10,000 to buy him back. Sam couldn't resist that much money so he took the offer. Lester wrote out a check for $5,000 and handed it to Sam along with Sam's check for

$5,000 which Sam had given him that morning. Lester led the horse away and Sam jumped in his truck and rushed to the bank and deposited Lester's check.

The next day, Sam decided he would trade with Lester again for the valuable horse so he went over and dickered with Lester until a trade was made for $20,000. Lester was shrewd and insisted that Sam give him two checks this time, one for $5,000 and one for $15,000. (Sam didn't know it but Lester was a director at the bank and knew of his bank account and the deposit of his check). While Sam led the horse back to his place, Lester headed to the bank and deposited the $5,000.

When Lester returned home, Sam was sitting on his front porch waiting for him. He had a bottle of bourbon in his hand and he appeared grief stricken. When he stepped upon the porch he could see tears streaming down Sam's cheeks and Sam blurted out" Old Bituminous died before I got home with him". Lester understood Sam's grief now and in minutes both grown men were crying, moaning and tilting the bourbon bottle. It was a sad occasion.

Sam finally said" Lester, me and you both loved that old horse and if he hadn't

of up and died, we both would have been rich by spring".

CHAPTER 8

AMOS, THE GRADING DOG

The school where all the scholars of the county attended was Caldwell County Consolidated High School (CCHS). The non scholars usually finished schooling at the eighth grade level at the many one room school houses around the county. They say that one of the unforgettable experiences of attending CCHS was to hear old "Professor" Beals tell how the algebra papers was graded. It seems that the professor lived in a two story house in Princeton and he had a little feist dog named Amos.

Dad's version of the story went something like this. Professor Beals said he had four rubber stamps custom made ~ one was A, one was B, one was C and the fourth was D. The professor would take the test papers home and place one paper on each step of the stairs to the second floor of his house. He would place a plate of food at the top of the stairs. Then he would tape the rubber stamps to Amos's feet, ink them up and set Amos down at the bottom of the stairs and let him climb the stairs to get the food.

Under this grading system, your grade depended upon which foot stepped on your paper. Over the years, I suppose it all averaged out and the professor didn't get too many complaints, at least not to his face for he was a stern man.

However, like all good things, the professors grading system finally came to an end. As Amos got to be an old fat dog, he couldn't make it all the way to the top of the steps without stopping a few times to sit down and rest. So many students began to complain about getting "O'S" that the professor had to abandon this grading system.

CHAPTER 9

TURPENTINE – A GOOD DOG MOVER

Back in the good old days, folks didn't take care of dogs like they do now. They didn't keep them locked up in fenced yards, keep them chained, and it was absolutely unheard of to have a dog in the house. Dogs just sort of knew where they belonged, and stayed there. They were fed table scraps to supplement what they caught to eat. There was always water around livestock so that was no problem. And they usually dug themselves a bed under the front porch or the corn crib for the warm months and slept in the barn or com crib in the cold months. All in all, they had the run of the place and were free - not a bad life.

However, ever now and then, dogs would get scattered some - an old witch dog would come in heat and take off across the country side with all the grown male dogs after her and this would upset natures balance. Pa Thomas use to describe this as "many were called - but few were chosen." Also, wandering dogs (called strays) might wander in and sort of settle down at somebody's place. As a consequence, sometimes the dog population would get too thick and the men folk would decide to solve the problem and have a little sport in the process, They would select an available barn, agree to round up all the stray dogs on a given day, and lock them in that barn for a session of "dog turpentining".

Somebody would bring a jug of turpentine and a sack of corn cobbs and they were ready for business.

Proper turpentining procedure required that someone catch a dog and bring him over by the barn door where two or three others would hold him while the applicator would pull his tail up and briskly rub a corn cob across his rectum until it was red and raw. At just the proper time, one of the holders would then splash turpentine on the area so prepared and they would crack the door wide enough for him to get through and turn him loose. By the time they released him he would be howling and his legs would be moving through second gear so when his feet hit the ground he was about to shift into high and he would fly through the door like a bullet.

The average dog wouldn't stop running until he was in the next county and some of the above average dogs made it as far as the state line - or so they say. Some dogs would lift up their hind legs and pull themselves across country with their front feet, scooting, so to speak on their hot rectums.

However inhumane this may sound to some of you little ole ladies; it worked. The dogs got redistributed and it was rare indeed when a turpentined dog returned to the county of his turpentining.

At one of these turpentining sessions they had about finished when Johnny "Fats" Akins came running up to the barn, huffing and puffing and all out of wind. When he got his breath he asked "Did you boys turpentine a little black and white cur dog with a collar on her?" Bill Haveland said "Yep, bout ten minutes ago". Fats said "I thought so, it looked like her streaking past the house a while ago and headed south towards Providence" .

Fats next dropped his pants and bent over and said" Turpentine me up good boys for I've got to catch her and bring her home. That was my wife's pet cur dog and if I can't catch her and bring her home, I'll be in the dog house for the rest of my borned days".

CHAPTER 10

THE BULLDOG AND THE MONKEY FIGHT

One of the exciting attractions in the rural way of life that got the juices flowing was a good dog fight. There might be a few dollars, pocket watches, knives, and dogs change hands based upon the outcome of the fight.

Therefore a good "fighting dog" was a prized possession and everyone tried to have one or two around the place - just in case the need arose. Josh Logan went a step further. He did some research and found out that the best fighting dogs were bulldogs.

So he slipped off on the train one day and went to Evansville, Indiana and bought himself the biggest , meanest bulldog he could find.

When he stepped off the train in Dawson and they unloaded the crate containing the big, bad bulldog the word spread like wildfire and practically everyone in town saw Josh's new fighting dog before he got out of town. What they saw was a big, vicious looking, magnificent animal. He was short and squatty looking with a chest the size of a whiskey barrel, wide as a barn door, and a fine set of choppers. When Josh loaded the crate on Lee Yates buggy he almost got dog bit.

Josh lived about eight miles east of town - right in the heart of the best "dog fighting" territory; and he had hardly got the bulldog uncrated before he was challenged by one of the Crockett boy's redbone hounds. To hear Josh tell the story, it wasn't much of a fight. The big bulldog got a grip on the hound and turned him every which way but loose and the fight was over.

Josh had a tendency to brag and to rub things in just a mite, and it didn't take him long to spread the word about his new fighter whipping heck out of the Crockett redbone (which up to then had been the local champion). It didn't take long for word to spread that Josh had the new champion fighting dog and that he would take on all challengers and cover all bets. As they say in the country, them was fightin words.

There was a challenge or two every week end from different fightin dogs around the county. Most of the dog fights were held out back of Baldy Cluck's store on the Ninth Vein road near where the bridge over the Tradewater river stood (the area was known also as the Clear Creek bottoms area). The only challenger who even gave the bulldog a run for his money was a big German Shepherd that a feller from Nebo brought over one Sunday afternoon. It seemed that the bulldog just got better and meaner with each victory and Josh got louder with his bragging and heavier in his pocketbook. By late summer things had become unbearable for the dog fighting fraternity and everyone was trying to figure out some way to beat that durned bulldog and that braggart Josh.

All summer long everyone had scoured the country side and bought or traded for every bad dog they could find. They had tried various hounds, birddogs, chows, collies. and German shepherds but the bulldog had whipped all comers. It appeared that he could not be beaten by another dog. And that is precisely what Shorty Roberts had figured out. But Shorty figured that he could be whipped and he proceeded with his bold plan.

Shorty had a first cousin that worked at the zoo in Louisville and he decided it was time to pay a visit to his city kinfolks so he caught the next east bound train out of Dawson and was gone for about two weeks. When he returned they unloaded a "mystery" crate off the train and loaded it on to Lee Yeats buggy and he and Shorty took it to Shorty's place near Cluck's store. It didn't take Shorty long to go over to Josh's place and challenge him to a showdown for the following Sunday afternoon. The word of the "showdown" had spread and there was a big crowd gathered at the "arena" on Sunday afternoon.

Josh arrived first and was busy mingling with the crowd and covering bets when Shorty finally arrived. He had the covered cage in his buggy. Josh had the mean bulldog on a stout lead chain and he walked over to Shorty's buggy, leading his bulldog. The bulldog hiked his hind leg and pissed on a buggy wheel then reared up on the buggy and smelled of the cage and commenced to growl - real mean and deep. Josh challenged Shorty to a bet but Shorty wanted odds. Josh said you can't be too proud of your dog, you even got him covered up so I can't even see him. By now a crowd had gathered around Shorty's buggy and Josh was really rubbing it in good. Shorty finally said "Ay gawd, tell you what I'll do you big blowhard - give me 10 to 1 odds and I'll bet a $50 gold piece".   Josh said" I'll take that easy money".

Shorty lifted the cover and opened the cage door and out jumped a monkey. The crowd let out a gasp then started laughing and Josh reared back and said "Heck fire Shorty, my bulldog will take one bite and your pore little monkey will be disappeared - this ain't a fair fight". The crowd roared again. Shorty said" In that case, you won't object if give my fighter a sharpened stick to defend himself with, will you?". Josh replied" Heck no, my bulldog can use it for a toothpick to pick his teeth with after he eats yore little old monkey. HA! HA! HA!" And the crown responded with more boisterous laughter.

Shorty took his monkey out into the ring and petted him and talked to him and handed him his "weapon". Meantime, Josh led the bulldog to the ring and unfastened the chain and held him by the collar and rubbed his stubby nose hard to make him mad. Shorty stood up and said "We're ready" and Josh yelled "Get the heck out of the way if you don't want to get eat up too by my monkey eating fighting bulldog" and he turned the bulldog loose.

The bulldog charged straight at the monkey, frothing at the mouth and fire in his eyes. Just before he got a bite of the monkey, it deftly leaped aside as the bulldog charged past. The bulldog charged three more times and each time the monkey jumped out of the way. One of the onlookers grabbed the monkey and the bulldog was able to get a big bite of his rump but another onlooker, think it was Magistrate Smith, whacked the bulldog on the nose with his walking stick and he let go.

By this time the monkey was mad and started chattering and showing its teeth and the bulldog charged again. Except this time, the monkey jumped straight up and came down on the dog's back facing to the rear. The monkey got a good grip and reached back and lifted the bulldog's stubby tail and commenced to jabbing him in the rectum with the sharpened stick. The bulldog just stood there and howled for a minute before he broke through the crowd and started running for the next county.

About every fifty yards the monkey would poke him in the rectum again with the bloody sharpened stick and the bulldog would let out a mournful wail and run faster. Soon, bulldog, monkey, and sharpened stick were out of sight and later out of sound. The crowd started laughing again, but for a different reason. Josh just stood there with his mouth open. Shorty approached Josh with his hand outstretched and Josh peeled off $500 and paid him in view of everyone. However, paying off the bet broke him and he announced to the others he would "pay them later - which he finally did", It broke Josh from ever bragging again too.

CHAPTER 11

OLE RIPPER

The "Ole Feller", Dick Short, was a real hound dog man. His favorite breed of hound was the Redbone; and through the years he had owned many redbone hounds which were famous locally for their ability to hunt down and tree the midnight bandits - the coons. They say, the Ole Feller would rather coon hunt than eat when he was hungry.

One time, one of the drummers who had stopped in Dawson to call on the local merchants, inquired around town if there were any coon hunters with good hounds in those parts. The drummer feller, who claimed to be a big coon hunter in his home country (somewhere up in Indiana), said he sure wanted to go coon hunting in West Kentucky while he was down in these parts ..

Almost everyone he talked to told him the same thing" Get in touch with the Ole Feller if you want to go on a real coon hunt". The drummer finally decided they weren't spoofing him so he found out how to get in touch with Mr. Short (better known as the Ole Feller). He rented a horse at the livery stable and rode out to Dick Short's farm. He got there right at sundown and when he rode up, the Ole Feller was just finishing up the chores- slopping the hogs, milking, etc. Ole Feller invited him to get down and stay a spell. The drummer slid off the horse and introduced himself and asked if a coon hunt was planned for tonight. The Ole

Feller's eyes lit up and he said "Why shore, when do you want to go". The drummer said "Right now".

The Ole Feller said "Unsaddle your horse and put him in the barn and we'll feed him some grain and throw down some hay for him. "After they had taken care of the horse the Ole Feller said "Let's go to the house and take this milk and I'll tell Maw where we're goin." Maw insisted they come in and eat supper and try some of the apricot fried pies she had made before they went trapsing off into the fool woods. Like obedient boys, they did as she said and were glad they did - the fried pies were excellent. They sat around the table and drank coffee and smoked cigarettes and got acquainted as it got dark outside.

Both men were starting to get a little anxious to go coon hunting and Ole Feller stood up and said "Let me put on my gum boots and get my carbide light and we'll get started - Did you bring boots and a light?" "No" responded the drummer so Old Feller said "Come on back with me and we'll see if! got anything that will fit you". They finally found an old pair of boots which fit and a spare carbide light - plus an old hunting coat. All set.

They went outside and the hound dogs were up and baying with tails switching before they got to the gate of the dog pen and turned three of them loose. All three were fine looking Redbone hounds and the drummer said as much. Ole Feller beamed and started bragging on them. He said, "Two of them are about the best hounds I ever hunted with - they be the two witches, Belle and

Bugle Ann. And that big stud dog is Belle's pup, Ole Ripper, and I think he is going to be the best coon hound that ever lived when he finishes growing up and gets rid of a couple of bad habits."

They lit up smokes and stood around awhile to let the dogs crap, piss and scratch a while before they finally headed toward the Boggy Creek bottoms for the hunt. The hounds trotted along with them till they got through the barnyard then they took off toward the woods. They had walked about a mile from the barn when the distinctive, clear voice of Belle rang out - ROW! ROW! ROWEE! Translated that meant "Folks, there's been a ring tail coon through here" and moments later the mellow voice of Bugle Ann and the deep bass voice of Ole Ripper joined in and that meant "and old ring tail was here not long ago and we're going to catch him". The chorus was now complete with the most beautiful hound dog music this side of heaven". At least it was beautiful to the Ole Feller and his guest hunter from Indiana who turned out to be a real coon hunter too, They speeded up their walk to keep the hound in hearing range.

After the three hounds got into high gear, the coon's fate was cast. There was no way he could outrun or outsmart these three pro's; so the old coon did what all hard pressed coons do - he climbed the tallest tree he could find. He felt secure in the tree and looked down at the hounds which were standing on hind legs with front legs resting on the tree and baying, as if at the moon. However, his feeling of security was short lived because he could see two lights bobbing through the woods and soon heard the hunters come crashing through the brush.

When the men got to the tree, Ole Ripper was going wild. He was actually trying to climb the tree and barking his fool head off. The Ole girls were sort of taking it easy and appeared to be smiling at the antics of the young stud dog, Ole Ripper.

The drummer from Indiana said "Them sure are fine coon hounds, Ole Feller. I never saw a hound as eager to get at a coon than Ole Ripper. I sure would like to see him tangle with a big Ole boar coon. By the way, how are we going to get the coon out of that tall tree?". The Ole Feller said" Well, I guess I'll try to shoot him out with my pistol if you hold the light for me". The drummer said" We don't ever shoot coons up in Indiana, we climb the tree and shake them out and watch a good coon fight". This stung the Ole Feller a bit and he pointed at the tree and said "Be my guest". The Hoosier immediately said" Aw heck, go ahead and shoot, I could never climb that tall tree" The Ole Feller handed him his light and pulled the pistol from his pocket and they backed away from the base of the tree and found a sapling for him to take a rest on and he aimed and fired "POW" Ole Feller would never admit it but he got off a lucky shot that just grazed the coon, and true to his prediction, the coon came climbing down the trunk real fast and leaped as far as he could out into the woods. But his leap was not far enough -

Ole Ripper caught him before he had taken a step. The other two dogs had been tied up before he shot because he was training Ole Ripper to fight a coon.

They had both lights shining on the coon and watched as Ole Ripper grabbed him by the nape of the neck and shook heck out of him. In seconds the coon's neck was broken and the coon fight was over - but not the action. Ole Ripper dropped the coon on the ground and seduced it quite thoroughly before he trotted off into the woods, looking for another coon. Ole Feller didn't say anything, he just untied Belle and Bugle Anne and they went racing off in the woods in the direction Ole Ripper had taken.

In less than fifteen minutes they hit another coon trail and the race was on again. They must have jumped this coon for they had him treed in no time. The results were the same, the big sow coon got it in the end by a big Redbone stud, just as the first coon had got it.

The Hoosier couldn't hold it any longer and he said "Ole Feller, how long has this been going on?" The Ole Feller said "Forever, I reckon" "Naw, naw, I mean how long has that Ripper dog been abusing coons like that?' The Ole Feller said "Ever since he was just a pup, that's the horniest animal I ever saw. I been afraid to break him of that bad habit, afraid he would lose interest in treeing coons if I did. I figure when he gets older, like me, he will break his own self'. "And besides, he seems to take such pleasure in that final act that I just sort of hate to take that part of the sport away from him" he concluded.

As the night wore on, they treed several more coons and all met the same fate - a broken neck and a thorough seducing by Ole Ripper.

Finally, the hounds got after a wise ole boar coon that took them on a long tough chase through the river bottoms. This ole coon had been chased many times before and he swam the river a couple of times before the hounds finally put him up a big beech tree right on the river bank. Ole Feller and the Hoosier finally reached the tree and the hounds were sitting on their haunches barking "treed". They shined their lights up in the tree and finally located the coon, lying on a big limb and peeping down at them ever so often. Ole Feller pulled out his pistol and tried to shoot at the coon but the gun had been broken in their scramble through the woods and would not fire. Ole Feller said" Let's leave this coon and head for the house, I'm all tuckered out". The Hoosier agreed, but suggested they let the hounds hunt on the way home. Ole Feller said "These Ole gals are tuckered too, I'll lead them but we'll let Ole Ripper run free and see if he trees anything else".

They headed back toward the house and just as they were leaving the bottoms and starting up a hill they heard Ole Ripper running a coon and he was headed right at them. Just before the coon got to the hunters Ole Ripper was nipping on his heels and he climbed the nearest tree, which wasn't very big and fairly easy to climb. The hunters got to the tree and saw the coon about 20 feet off the ground. Ole Feller said "Aw heck, that's a young coon, let's leave him for seed". The

Hoosier said" Naw, if you don't mind I'd like to see one more performance by Ole Ripper and I can darn sure climb this little tree" Ole Feller said" Get to climbing"

The Hoosier started up the tree and about the time he got to the coon, it climbed higher to the very top of the tree with the Hoosier right behind it. The Hoosier was so intent on knocking the coon out of the tree that he got careless and climbed on a small limb that snapped with his weight.

As the Hoosier came tumbling and falling through the limbs he regained his senses enough to scream out "HOLD OLE RIPPER".

CHAPTER 12

THE VIRILE ROOSTER

Virility was the theme of many of the stories told among the men folk. This subject always made a good story. Today, these stories are sometimes referred to as "dirty jokes" although they are not near as "dirty" as the stuff kids are exposed to on TV and in the movies on a daily basis. Back then, they were just "men stories". This particular story was one of Paw Thomas' favorites.

Moon Quigley had a big flock of laying hens and for years he had been the biggest egg producer in the county. He crated eggs and shipped them by rail all the way to Saint Louis. One year his egg production started to fall off real bad and he started to short ship eggs on his contract to the buyer in Saint Louis. It really started to worry Moon and he discussed it with his wife who said "I'll bet it is caused by them dad blamed hawks that fly over the chicken coop and scare them poor old hens so bad they can't lay eggs". Moon started keeping his rifle handy and every time he saw a hawk, he took a shot at it. Soon the hawks became scarce around the Quigley chicken farm - but egg production fell off further.

Moon started feeding more but nothing happened. He was desperate and he told the boys at the Whittle and Spit Club at Oranges store of his problem. Schrethie Orange overheard him and said "Moon, I hear there's a new animal doctor over at Hoptown, they call him a "vegetarian" or something like that. I'll bet he could solve your problem".   Moon said "I'm ready to try anything, do you think he would come all the way out to my place to check on my hens?"'. "Why sure" replied Schrethie, "the next time someone

comes through here headed for Hopkinsville, I'll send word that you need his services - but it will cost you maybe $20 dollars". Moon replied" If he gets the hens to laying again that will be a bargain".

Several days later, Moon was outside cleaning out the hen house when he heard a Model A drive up and stop in front of his house. He walked toward the car and this young feller climbed out and extended his hand and said "Howdy, I'm Doctor Lovell - hear you got some sort of problem with your chickens". "I'm real proud to make your acquaintance Doctor and I sure enough got serious problems" replied Moon. Moon led him to the chicken coop and they stepped inside the gate. The young doctor immediately

caught one of the hens and examined her and started asking questions in rapid fire order "How long ago did egg production fall off? Had he changed their feed rations? Had any of the hens appeared sick? Had any of them died? etc." Moon answered his questions and the doctor said" There's nothing wrong with this hen and quite frankly, I'm puzzled" Lets step inside the hen house and let me examine a couple more" They did.

They went back outside and the doctor said " Mr. Quigley, there is nothing wrong with your hens, matter of fact, I have never seen any more healthy. Let's take a look at your roosters?" Moon said "Roosters? What roosters? I ain't got but one. Had two others but they got into a big fight and one killed the other and a fox got the crippled up survivor." The doctor asked "Where is the one you got left?". Moon said "He usually hangs out down at the barn". The doctor said" Let's go catch him and let me examine him". "OK" said Moon and started toward the barn.

When they got to the barn they looked around and finally located the old rooster on the shady side of the barn. He was leaning up against the side of the barn. The doctor exclaimed "There's your problem, I don't even need to examine him. That's the sorriest looking rooster I ever laid eyes on. Obviously he's too old to cut the mustard anymore, matter of fact he looks near death, naw, he looks like death warmed over."

Moon looked at the old rooster for a minute and said "By golly Doc, I think you hit the nail on the head. I been so worried about the hens that I completely forgot about the rooster. What should I do?".

The Doc answered " You've got to get a good, virile young rooster to service those hens. Matter of fact, I'm headed to Crofton right now and Jake Evans, who lives just north of Crofton, has some fine dominicker roosters. I'd be happy to stop and get you one and bring him back by here in a day or two - he'd probably sell the best one he's got for $10 and I could add it to my bill. Moon said" How much is your bill?". The young Doctor said I'm going to charge you $15 for this call. Moon went inside the house and returned and said, "Would you settle for a twenty dollar bill for this call plus the young rooster?". The doctor stuck his hand out and said "Done" and took the money.

Sure enough, true to his word, the doctor drove up in his Model A Ford three days later. Moon went out to the car and as he walked up the doctor removed a small cage from the back seat and proudly showed the rooster to him. Moon said" My goodness, ain't he a dandy, don't think I ever seen a bigger more healthier looking rooster than that gentleman" .

The doctor handed the cage to Moon and said "Just open the cage door and you will see some action from this rooster ... .I guarantee". Sure enough, when Moon opened the door, the young rooster marched out, ruffled his feathers, scratched around a time or two, and reared back and let go with a loud COCK-A-DOODLE-DO! and headed straight to the hen house.

The hens were sure glad to see him and they promptly lined up to receive his service. He went down the line, and one by one provided each one with that which she had long been missing. All the hens started clucking and making such a commotion over the action that had just transpired that all the fowl on the farm started toward the hen house. Here came several guineas, ducks, and geese. One thing about this rooster, he didn't discriminate - he proudly serviced all the

- 60 -

guineas, ducks and geese - then strutted around for a while and crowed some. It appeared he had run out of customers.

The Doc and Moon had been observing all this activity and the Doc said "Well Mr. Quigley, I believe your egg production is solved". While he said this the rooster started marching up a small hill beside the hen house and both watched in amazement as the rooster started across the top of the hill and fell over on his back and spread his wings. Moon said "Dad gum it, he over did it and done suicide his self. It looks to me like my problem was only temporarily solved. Are you gonna give me a refund?". "Just wait a minute and don't go jumping to any hasty conclusions" replied the doctor.

They stood around a minute and talked and Moon looked toward the hill and exclaimed "Hasty conclusions my hind end, the buzzards is already circling that dad gum dead rooster, I'm gonna get a shovel and go bury him".

Moon got the shovel and they started up the hill. Just before they stepped out on the top of the hill, the doctor grabbed Moon by the arm and stopped him and pointed toward the rooster.

A couple of buzzards were almost low enough to land and others were on their way down. The rooster was still on his back and cocked his head so he was looking at Moon and he had a toe on his bill (making the keep quiet sign) and was also winking at Moon. Moon exclaimed "Well I'll be dab blamed, he ain't dead"'. "Naw,'" said the Doc, "He's just trying to lure them buzzards down for a little of his fine service".

CHAPTER 13

JUST IDENTIFYING MYSELF - "THAT'S ALL"

Paw Thomas could hardly wait for Dad to finish his pill story so he could tell this one about the scrawny old bull.

Milton "Pinch" Capps raised a few beef cattle and he had a little white faced red bull that he had owned for several years. For the past couple of years, his calf crop had fallen off and he had tried the vet and the little black pills but they didn't work with his little bull.

One day, Pinch was in Orange's store and he was complaining about his calf crop (or lack thereof). Pinch was tight with his money and complained about everything. He got around to complaining about wasting his money with the vet. Finally, Joe Lisanby had heard enough and he lit into old Pinch. "Darn it Pinch, everybody in the county knows why you ain't getting no calves. That darn little old white face bull of yours is too old to cut the mustard anymore. The vet told you that and so has everybody else you've complained to. I've got a good young bull I'd sell to you for $100 cash money and would even deliver him to you".

Pinch whined "Joe, you know I ain't got that kind of money to spend". Joe said "Horse apples - you've got enough folding paper money to burn a wet elephant with and enough gold buried in your smokehouse to re-stock Fort Knox" .. All eyes in the store were on Pinch after Joe got through with him.

Pinch, as much in an effort to escape as anything, said "OK Joe." Joe snapped "Ok what?"

Pinch said "OK Mr. Lisanby, you bring that young bull to my place, and if he gets the job done, I'll pay you $75 for him. Joe replied" Pinch, you ain't only gettin old - you are gettin deaf too - I said $100. Pinch said" Oh, I forgot, bring him over in the morning and I'll pay the $100 you ask - providing he does the job."

The next morning Pinch heard Joe yelling "Open the durn gate- I've brought the bull". Pinch rushed outside and rushed down to the barn and opened the gate to the pasture, then helped Joe. herd the young bull through the gate and out into the pasture which was full of passionate and ready cows.

The very first thing that the young bull did was march straight to the nearest cow, walk around her one time, then mount and "service" her. As soon as he finished this assignment, he walked over to the next nearest cow and repeated the performance. By now, the other cows and heifers in the pasture figured out what was going on so they all walked over to where the young bull was and lined up. The young bull started down the line and one by one "serviced" each cow and heifer - he even back tracked and "serviced
a couple of the prettier young heifers twice. Pinch watched in amazement and when Joe thrust out his hand, palm up, Pinch counted out $100 in ten dollar bills and placed them in the palm.

While Pinch was paying for the young bull, the bull was casually walking to the back corner of the pasture where Pinch's little old white faced bull was standing under a shade tree and had been observing the services. As the young bull drew nearer to the old bull, the old bull started running his thing out. The young bull saw this and said to the old bull "What do you think you're going to do with that thang old bull?" "Nothing Boss" the old bull responded, "I'm just identifying myself, that's all".

CHAPTER 14

GOT THE DEAD WOOD ON YOU NOW

Uncle Josh White use to tell the following story at every opportunity. Uncle Josh was almost 100 years young and claimed he remembered the days when eagles really did soar in Kentucky skies.

The old eagle was nearly starved and barely able to fly. He had been soaring over hill and dale for days, trying to catch a rabbit or squirrel or anything to eat - but without any success. If he didn't get something to eat soon, he would die. He decided to try to catch a fish in the Tradewater river - that might be easier to do.

The old eagle found a perch, high in an old dead beech tree on the river bank. He sat there and watched the river, hoping to see a fish, snake --anything to eat -- doggone, he was about starved to death.

Directly, the old eagle saw this long black eel casually swimming along in the shallow water near the river bank. The eagle swooped down off his high perch and caught the eel in his talons. He flew back to the bank and ate the eel. He then started to fly back to his high perch and before he got there, the eel slithered through him and out of his rectum and fell back into the river. The eagle flew back to his perch and sat dejectedly and hungrier than ever.

The eel, pleased with his performance, moved back into the shallow water and continued swimming lazily down the river, with no fear from the predator. The eagle got a glimpse of the eel and decided to try to catch him again and he dove off the limb in a dive aimed directly at the long black eel. He hit the target and was soon flying back toward the bank, a long black eel securely in his grasp.

This time the old eagle did not land directly on the bank; instead he landed on an old dead tree stump. He ate the eel and sat down flat on the stump and confidently stated "I've got the dead wood on you now".

CHAPTER 15

TALKING TO THE ANIMALS

Even back in the good old days, some of the young bucks left their homes in the backwoods of Kentucky and went out into the world to seek their fortunes. One such adventuresome type was Wash Evans (George Washington Evans, but Wash for short).Wash left home the day he turned 21 and caught the first freight train out of Dawson. He didn't get off the freight train until it reached its destination - Chicago. Wash didn't have any particular destination in mind when he left home - it just happened

that Chicago was the rail "hub" for that part of the country and that's where he ended up.

He wandered around the big city for several days on foot and slept in parks. He finally got a job as a dishwasher in a Greek restaurant and found a room in a flea bag boarding house nearby. This wasn't exactly what he had in mind when he left the farm; so after he sort of got the lay of the land he started looking for something better and got a job in a meat packing plant. Although the pay was much better, Wash allowed later that the working conditions weren't much better.

One night Wash went to a burlesque show and made a significant discovery - he was a natural born ventriloquist. The discovery was made when the featured entertainer that night, a ventriloquist, called for a volunteer from the audience and Wash volunteered. The performer proceeded to make a monkey out of Wash because he used Wash as his "Dummy" and would throw his voice and have Wash say silly, funny, and downright stupid things. Anyway, the audience applauded and liked the show. The performer told Wash if he would come backstage after the show he would give him a couple of bucks.

Wash went backstage and found the performer and told him he would rather learn how to do the trick than have the money. The performer showed Wash how to throw his voice and darned if Wash didn't learn how to do it in a couple of minutes. The performer was amazed and Wash thanked him and left.

Old Wash was no dummy and he went back to the boarding house and practiced throwing his voice. He could see all kinds of possibilities of some fun later on, if he got good enough. He would sit in his room and make the chair talk, the lamp talk, etc. Then he would go outside and if a stray cat or dog wandered by he would make them talk. He really got a kick out of watching peoples reaction to the talking dogs and cats.

But he had the most fun with his new found skill at work. He would get to work early and wander around the packing plant and make the carcasses talk. For example, in the slaughter pen he would have the cow or hog yell "Please don't kill me, I'll give you all my money if you spare me". - or around the butcher area he would have the carcass yell "OUCH" when the butchers cut off a cut of meat.

Many of the workers were immigrants and Wash was literally scaring the bejabbers out of them.

Wash was having an effect on the output of the plant and management was upset. They finally caught him in the act and fired him. Wash was back on the street, looking for work. By now he felt that dishwashing jobs and such were beneath his skills so he couldn't find a job to suit him. He had saved most of the money he earned and decided it was time to return home for a surprise visit to the folks. He could hop a freight train and the trip wouldn't cost much. He purchased a cheap carpet bag and packed a few things, including some cheap gifts for the folks, and went to the rail yards. He checked around with the "hobos" and found a freight headed for Kentucky and slipped aboard along with an old hobo.

The next day the train stopped, and the hobo said they were in Louisville, and would soon depart for Atlanta. Wash hopped off and finally located a freight with Illinois Central empty coal cars which he figured must be headed for West Kentucky and Dawson - and it was. When the train began to roll westward, Wash boarded it. A few hours later it pulled off on a siding at the Dawson Daylight Mines to spot some coal cars, and Wash unboarded. He walked to the mines and waited for shift change where he spotted Lumus Cole who he had grown up with and who lived up on the Cadiz hill road - and who owned a Model A Ford. He bummed a ride to his folks place with Lumus. It was nearly dark when Lumus let him off at the farm. Mrs. Evans looked out the window when she heard the car stop out front and exclaimed "Lordy Mercy, I think Wash is home". About that time the front door opened and Wash stepped inside and Mr. Evans said "Aye Gawd, it is Wash his self". They all embraced and everyone started talking at once. They finally settled down into a question and answer session with Wash providing

the answers to his parent's questions.

Wash finally got away from the questions by unpacking his carpet bag and passing out presents. The most popular gifts were a case knife for his pappy, an apron with a picture and "the World's Fair" printed on it for his mammy and a rag doll for his kid sister, Susie. Wash was the family hero and considered a great success and they sat up late that night listening to the wild tales that Wash spun about the wonderful city of Chicago. They couldn't believe a city could be that big. They finally went to bed.

The next morning, Wash woke up to the wonderful aroma of bacon frying and coffee perking, and despite the strong temptation to roll over and go back to sleep, he slipped into his clothes and went into the kitchen to get a cup of coffee, snitch a piece of bacon, and join the family for breakfast. He had almost forgotten how good a country breakfast was. Kings in Europe didn't eat as well as country folk.

After breakfast, Mr. Evans invited Wash to accompany him to the barn to milk and do the chores. Wash dutifly tagged along. When they got to the barn and Wash saw the old cow standing there, waiting to be milked and fed, he couldn't resist the urge to pull a prank on the old man. He said "Pappy, one thing I didn't tell y'all last night was that I learned to talk to animals while I was up to Chicago city". Mr. Evans said" Go on boy, you don't expect me to believe that do you? And some of the stuff you said last night sounded sort of farfetched as well".

He added" I think what you really learned in Chicago was how to tell tall tales".   He sat down on the stool and started to milk the old cow. Wash said "What if I talk to the old cow and she talks back, would you believe me then?" Mr. Evans said "Son, I've been milking this old cow since she first came fresh as a heifer, and if she could talk, she'd a said something to me long afore now"

Wash said "Hello Mrs. Cow. How has pappy been treating you?'. The cow replied "Oh, purty good in general, except sometimes he short changes me on my feed.   And another thing, on cold mornings his hands are like icicles when he grabs a hold of my teats and starts milkin". Pappy was aghast and nearly fell off the milkin stool- but he didn't say a thing - apparently he wasn't upset with her answer.

Wash then spoke to the horse that was in the adjoining stall. "Mr. Horse, do you have anything you want to say about the way pappy treats you?". The horse replied "Why yes, he has always been purty good to me and kept my stall clean and full of clean straw; he feeds me lots of corn, especially when I'm working and sometimes he even brags about me to the neighbors. But, on the other hand, he sometimes forgets and leaves me outside in cold, damp weather; and sometimes he has me pulling loads that two

mules shouldn't have to pull". By now, pappy was stupefied and bewildered. But he remained silent.

About that time a sheep walked into the hallway of the barn and they both saw her at the same time. Wash said "Hello Mrs. Sheep, how does Pap ... " Pappy interrupted him before he finished the question and said" Now Wash, don't you believe a word she says. That's the lieingist sheep I ever owned".

CHAPTER 16

THE CREAMED CAT

Every rural area out of necessity had a blacksmith. Good, bad, or indifferent, he was an essential part of the rural economy and usually held a monopolistic position.

Harve Pool was an enormous man who was virtually the king of the Cerulean Springs area. In addition to owning the only general store for miles, he also owned a grist mill, a sorghum mill, and the only blacksmith shop in the area. He was what you would call "The tycoon of the backwoods".

Harve was a rough and tumble man and usually very loud and boisterous. He chewed tobacco and cussed a lot, particularly when shooing mules and horses. It was rumored that he kept a hickory pole handy and would whack a mule between the ears before he started to shoe him - just to get his attention. Most of the men folk didn't like Harve - they feared him physically and economically. The women folk didn't like him either - probably for about the same reasons.

Harve's wife Pearl, on the other hand, was just the opposite. She was quiet, shy, and gentle. She bore him fourteen kids and I suppose that would make any woman sort of shy at least. One of her faults, which Harve was forever ranting and raving about, was that she was a terrible housekeeper. They said her house hadn't been clean since the day it was built. It always smelled of babies - urine, poo-poo, etc, There were always dirty dishes on the table, dirty pots on the stove, beds unmade, dirty clothes in every corner, etc. Harve never got use to the dirty house and did his best to keep visitors out of it.

My dad tells about the time he was sent to Harve's blacksmith shop to get a horse shod. He stood around and watched and accidently backed into Harve's forge and burned his arm severely. Naturally, he let out a squall that could be heard for miles and started crying. Pearl came running out of the house and to the blacksmith shop to see what had happened (Dad thinks she thought it was one of her kids that was hurt - she had so many she couldn't keep track of them). In the meantime, Harve told dad to shut up - said it wasn't much of a burn; and had got a glob of axle grease and was about to rub it on the wound when Pearl came through the door and yelled at him to stop.

She took dad by the hand and led him to the house to doctor him up proper. Harve followed them to the house, bickering and blabbering all the way that it was just a little ole burn and nothing serious. (Dad thinks he didn't want him to see the messy house).

Anyway, Pearl led dad into the kitchen, got some freshly churned butter, and gently rubbed it onto the wound. Next, she took a sheet and tore some strips from it and wrapped his arm and made a neat bandage. By now, dad had quit crying and had regained his composure.

Pearl had been churning buttermilk when the accident happened and the chum was still sitting by the kitchen table. She offered dad a glass of fresh buttermilk and some cornbread which he accepted - it had been a long time since breakfast.

When Pearl went to the churn to ladle out a glass of buttermilk for dad she exclaimed" My goodness" and gently lifted out a near drowned kitten which had fallen into the churn. "Poor kitty" said Pearl as she held the kitten by the nape of the neck and stripped the buttermilk from its fur and into the churn. She set the kitten on the floor and filled his glass with buttermilk, as if nothing had happened.

Dad went home with a burned arm and an upset stomach.

CHAPTER 17

THE BLUE RIBBON COW

The Illinois central railroad cut across the back side of the Jim Ed Smith place. Old Jim Ed didn't like it being there and was always threatening to hire some city lawyers and make the railroad company move its track. He claimed the trains were too noisy and kept him awake and they were a danger for his livestock.

Of course, the railroad people didn't pay any attention to him, the rails had been laid before Jim Ed had even been born. And it was known by all in the county that Jim Ed's livestock was some of the scrubbiest in that end of Kentucky.

However, as fate would have it, one day a train came through and one of Jim Ed's cows was on the track and the steam engine made hamburger out of her. The railroad representative found a piece of rope near the scene of the accident and the railroad contended that Jim Ed had intentionally tied the old cow to the rails. Jim Ed did hire lawyers on this and it came to trial.

While Jim was on the witness stand and being questioned, he was asked to describe the animal which had been hit by the train. Jim Ed stuttered a minute and blurted out" I ga ga got a bunch of sorry cattle on my place your honor and had one prize jersey cow that won the blue ribbon at the county fair - and that

darn railroad bunch picked out my $1,000 blue ribbon cow to run over".

CHAPTER 18

THE FIRST CONSULTANT

Buford Tinsley owned the bank in Princeton, as well as the insurance agency and a sawmill. He was an old bachelor and sort of tight with his money - and folks said he had plenty. Paddle foot Edison used to say "Shucks fire, Buford's got enough money to stack up, climb on top of it - and see Dawson," if that gives you a clue as to his rank and smell. He was boss everywhere, except at home.

Buford had an old black (with a white tipped tail) tomcat that lived in the house with him. He had raised the cat from a kitten and was quite fond of it. But the cat had begun to sort of aggravate Buford because every night about dark, the tomcat would get up from his cat box, stretch, yawn, and go to the door and start scratching and meowing - wanting out. Buford would have to stop whatever he was doing and go let the cat out. The tomcat would stay out all night and show up outside Buford's window about daylight, meowing and wanting back inside. He woke Buford up every morning.

Buford thought, why should my life be controlled by that bad blamed old cat? Am I not the boss? A few days later the new veterinarian was in the bank, making a deposit, and Buford called him into his office for some "free" advice. He described his problem with the tomcat and the vet said "Mr. Tinsley, if you want to bring the cat to my office tomorrow around 10 o'clock, I think I can cure your problem". Buford asked "How much will it cost?" The doctor said "$30" and Buford said "I'll be there".

The next morning Buford took the cat to the vet and the vet performed surgery on him. (castration, in case you were wondering). Buford took the tomcat back to the house and put him in the cat box. That night when it got dark, the cat didn't stir, he just slept. For about three more weeks the cat stayed near his box and didn't even notice when it got dark. Buford bragged all over Princeton on the new vet. But the "solution" was short lived - the tomcat reverted to his old habits.

Buford caught the young vet in the bank in a few days and raised cane with him. The vet was embarrassed and very uncomfortable. Finally, Buford asked "Dr. Lovell, you are fresh out of school and so durned smart; how do you explain my tomcats behavior?". The vet shifted from foot to foot and thought for a minute and responded " As best I can tell, your durned old tomcat has become a consultant".

C. POLITICS, RELIGION, MEDICINE, AND THE LAW

Everyone knew better, but when two or more country folk got together they sooner or later got into a discussion about politics or religion. Off times, these discussions would lead to fights or even bloodshed. And bloodshed led to doctors and medicine and then to lawsuits and lawyers.

But Kentuckians have a good sense of humor and most of the times before these discussions reached the stage of violence, someone would tell a story based on one of these subjects. A few that I recall include:

Chapter

19   The Best Political Speech Ever Made

20   Faith vs. Knowledge

21   Firearm On My Hip

22   Little Black Pills

23   Some Prayers Are Answered

24   Medical Advice - Worth What it Cost

25   Seen Us

CHAPTER 19

THE BEST POLITICAL SPEECH

Granddad Thomas dabbled in politics all his adult life and from time to time ran for minor county offices - justice of the peace, magistrate, etc. He was a staunch Democrat (as were most of the West Kentuckians in those days), and his voting decisions were quite simple; he would always vote Democrat and never vote Hipocrat (that was his category for Republicans and all others). This is a story told about the first race he ever ran.

According to Uncle Josh White, the local farmers were quite upset with the incumbent magistrate and had decided that Granddad would make an acceptable replacement. Several of them approached him to convince him to run for the office and he really didn't want to do it. However, after several visits and about a gallon of sippin whiskey, they finally coaxed him into running for magistrate. Charlie Ely drove him to the county seat and helped him fill out the papers or whatever to run the race. He took Granddad back home and that was about the end of it. Granddad didn't campaign or anything - he just announced he was a candidate.

His opponent, the incumbent, was a merchant in Princeton and was very actively campaigning for reelection. About every fence post in the county had his poster tacked on it. In addition, everyone who entered his store received a free box of matches with his name and picture on it. The group of supporters who had talked Granddad into running for office were getting concerned because Granddad wasn't actively campaigning. They sent a representative, again Charlie Ely, by to talk to him. Granddad said "Heck fire Charlie, you know I didn't want to make this race, if you boys want any campaigning done, you all do it".

Charlie reported back to the committee and they had a pow wow to decide what action to take. They finally decided to lure Granddad to Princeton the next first Monday when all the farmers would be in town and have him make a political speech.

Again, the task fell to good ole Charlie, so on the next first Monday he went by Granddad's place and picked him up in his buggy and hauled him to Princeton and they were met at the wagon yard by the committee. The wagon yard was packed with people and a fiddler was up in a wagon bed, playing music. There were a few signs tacked up announcing Granddad's upcoming speech. Other politicians had been making speeches off and on all that day. Charlie led Granddad to the wagon and explained that he was expected to make a political speech. Granddad objected and wasn't going to do it but slick talking Charlie convinced him that he only had to make this one speech and everyone would be happy. Granddad finally said" All right, I'll make just this one speech and she's gonna be a short one". Charlie said that was fine.

Granddad climbed up in the wagon bed and Charlie climbed up beside him and rattled and rang a cow bell to get everyone's attention. The crowd finally gathered around the wagon and settled down. Charlie made a short introduction then hopped to the ground and left Granddad to face the audience.

Granddad shuffled his feet, looked out over the audience, cleared his throat, and made the following classic political speech:

"Folks" he said, " I know most of you and most of you know me. I didn't want to make this race but some of my neighbors sort of talked me into it. I ain't no politician and I ain't no speech maker. This is the only political speech I'm gonna make so listen good. " This got everyone's attention and they got very quiet and attentive. Then he said" If all of you will line up and drop your drawers, I'll come down the line and kiss everyone's hind end that promises to vote for me". A gigantic gasp came from the audience and they got quiet again. Granddad paused then concluded, "But if I'm elected, all of you can kiss mine".

CHAPTER 20

FAITH VS. KNOWLEDGE

The country folk took their religion seriously. All of the older preachers realized this and the young preachers who came from the preacher school in Nashville soon figured it out. The congregations weren't interested in all that theology and other stuff they didn't understand; they wanted a dose of heck fire and darnation illustrated by examples they could relate to.

I always figured that the parables in the Bible were written especially for West Kentuckians. They loved and understood those stories that made and illustrated a moral point.

One Sunday, the Reverend Joe David Simpkins was preaching the sermon at the Macedonia Hard Shell Baptist church. His subject was "Faith". Joe David hadn't been out of the seminary more than three months and he had gotten himself all bogged down trying to explain the difference between religious faith and scientific knowledge. His congregation was starting to stir around and was getting very restless. If it would have been a ball game they would have been booing him.

Elder Eddie Shear decided he had better save this poor young minister so he stood up and announced it was time for a good gospel and told Sister Eudena Percy to play "When the Saints go Marching In" (key of C) and Eddie got them started with the song. Then Eddie walked up to the pulpit and got Joe David aside and told him he would have to think of an example the folks would understand to illustrate the point he was trying to make, then Eddie went back to his seat.

Joe David was racking his brain for a simple illustration as the congregation sang and he looked out over the congregation and finally saw his answer - right there on the front row. The song ended and Joe David let out a loud "Praise the Lord".

Then he reared back and in his loud and deep voice he said "Folks, I've been preaching to you this morning about Christian faith and I'm afraid I mixed in too much scientific knowledge in the process. He continued, There is a whale of a difference betwixt the two".

He paused for effect and said, " Let me illustrate the difference. Mr. & Mrs. Carter are with us this morning with their eight lovely children. They are seated down there in the front row -- would you mind standing up please. The Carter family dutifly stood up and faced the congregation. Then the Reverend Joe David made his point. "Fellow Christians he said, this lovely couple has eight lovely children. Mr. Carter thinks they are all his - that's Faith. On the other hand, Mrs. Carter knows that all of them are hers -- that's Knowledge"

The service drew to a close and everyone went home happy and Joe David became a popular preacher and a successful one after that.

CHAPTER 21

FIREARM ON MY HIP

William (Wild Bill) Higgins had been a deputy Sheriff in Hopkins County all of his adult life (which could be good-or bad). Sheriff Jim Kirk Nester died and Judge Harlan appointed Wild Bill acting sheriff to complete the unexpired term.

When election time rolled around, Wild Bill announced his candidacy for sheriff. He campaigned as good as he knew how. He made speeches, went from door to door shaking hands and kissing babies, etc. His opponent was an out of work Baptist preacher named Sol Minor. Sol campaigned hard too and made lots of promises and "deals".

On election day when the votes were counted the results were:

Sol Minor - 2,165   William Higgins - 5

The next day Tom Sisk ran into Wild Bill at the Purina Feed Store in Nortonville and Wild Bill was wearing a six -shooter on his hip. Tom asked him "William, why are you packing a gun, you ain't the law no more".

Wild Bill looked him right in the eye and said "Aye gawd, with no more friends than I got in this county, I've got to tote a gun".

CHAPTER 22

LITTLE BLACK PILLS

If Dad was around when Paw Thomas told the rooster story, he had to jump in and tell this story about the horse with the virility problem.

John Turner, from the Piney Grove area, had a big black Morgan stud horse that he had owned for several years. The big Morgan was the daddy of most colts born in that end of the county for the past fifteen years or so. John usually charged a stud fee of $5 or let his friends and close neighbors use the service for free.

Cletus Jones had brought his mare down for service and nothing happened. He told John about the problem and recommended he have a vet come by and check him out. John said "Naw, I ain't gonna spend my money on no vet, if he can't cut the mustard no more he can join the crowd of us old folks and do without". Cletus asked "Mind if I bring the vet by, I'll pay for it". John said "If you want to waste your money, go ahead".

Cletus left his mare in the pasture with the stud and went and got Doc Lovell and brought him out. The Doc checked the stud and decided he could be cured. He left a bottle of little black pills with John and told him to put two of the pills in the oats every time he fed the horse. John got a bucket of oats and gave him his first dose while the Doc and Cletus were still there. Nothing happened and they left but Cletus left the mare.

The next morning when John woke up he heard the horses whining and he got up and looked out. The horses were running around the pasture like colts and now and then they would stop and the Morgan would rear up on Cletus' mare and do his duty.   After breakfast, John fed the stud another bucket of oats and put four little black pills in it this time. Cletus came by later and John told him about what he had observed. Cletus said "I told you that vet could fix him up". Cletus took his mare and left.

Later in the day, John looked out in the pasture and didn't see his stud horse. He rushed out to find out what had happened and found the front fence down and saw the horse's tracks. He was headed west. John followed the tracks down the muddy road to where he had gone through his neighbors fence across the road. John climbed through the fence and sure enough, his horse was over in the edge of the woods playing with a little strawberry roan mare. In moments he mounted her. When he was finished, John

caught him and led him home, put him in the barn, and patched the fence.

On Saturday, he was at Oranges store and got to talking with a few of his neighbors and told them of the miracle which that new Doc Lovell had performed with them little black pills. Rufus Ausen boy said " Well I'll swear, that was a miracle; wonder what's in them little black pills?'

John studied a minute before answering, then he drawled "Don't rightly know, but they taste a lot like licorice".

CHAPTER 23

SOME PRAYERS ARE ANSWERED

Ask and it shall be given ....

The widow Maude Brown didn't get religion until a couple of years after Sam was killed by the Feds while tending his still. It was claimed to be a work related accident. Maude had been a rounder in her teens and had a few real good times after Sam's untimely departure (but before she got religion).

Maude went to the tent revival in Crabtree and got an extra strong dose of religion one summer. And there ain't nothing more religious than a reformed sinner.

That Monday afternoon, her neighbor, Claudine Gasket, stopped by Maude's house to leave some quilting material that she had promised to bring her. Claudine knocked on the door but none answered. The door was unlocked so Claudine went inside and placed the material on the kitchen table. She called Maude's name several times - still no answer. She looked out the back door and saw a churn by the steps and figured that Maude might be down at the barn milking so she started toward the barn. Before she got to the barn she heard Maudine. Her voice would rise then soften so Claudine stopped and listened to see what she was saying and heard Maude praying.

"Rain down rocks on all the sinners Lord......Rain down rocks on the sinners... Hallelujah! Praise the Lord..... Bless his Holy name...."

Claudine thought for a minute and sort of sized up the situation and decided to sort of give the Lord a helping hand. She figured that Maude must be just outside the back door to the barn, down on her knees praying. She knew the barn had a hay loft so she gathered up an apron full of rocks and climbed up in the barn hay loft and slipped to the far end of the barn and looked down. Just as she had guessed, Maude

was on her knees praying and Maude said one more time "Lord, dear Lord, rain down rocks on the sinners" and as she completed her request, Claudine dumped her apron full of rocks on Maude's head.

Maude jumped up and shouted toward the heavens "Scatter'em out some Lord, scatter'em out".

CHAPTER 24

FREE MEDICAL ADVICE - WORTH WHAT IT COST

Pullet Edison raised chickens and sold eggs and fryers to the town folk in the towns in the area. (This was way before frozen foods were invented and before the outbreak of the major poultry producers in Arkansas, Missouri, Texas, etc.) In West Kentucky when you thought of chickens you thought of Pullet Edison and vice versa.

The local farmers considered the young vet that had recently set up his practice in Hoptown to be a horse and cow doctor and didn't figure he would mess with chickens. Everyone did his or her own chicken doctoring and the standard medicines used were turpentine, kerosene, sulphur, cod liver oil, mineral oil, and Watkins's liniment. They all thought that just about any chicken (or any animal) sickness could be cured with one or the other of these "medicines" - or a combination thereof.

One winter, Pullets hens quit laying eggs. They just sat on the roost or milled around the hen house all day. They would hardly eat. Pullet tried all of the remedies he could think of - at least all that had worked in the past. No improvement.

He went to the feed store in Princeton and told the owner of his problem. The owner said that he believed that Jess Claxton had a similar problem a while back and suggested that Pullet might go by and talk to Jess. So Pullet did.

He stopped by Jess's place and found Jess slopping his hogs. He went out to talk to him. "Yes" said Jess, "My hens got to acting just like you described yours are acting" .. Pullet figured he had discovered pay dirt so he eagerly asked "What did you give em Jess?" Jess looked him square in the eye and said" Pullet, I tell you what I fed my old hens - was carbide" "CARBIDE" exclaimed Pullet, "I'd a never thought of that" He thanked Jess, shook his hand, and left and went straight to O'Bryan's hardware store and bought five pounds of carbide. (Carbide was in abundance in that area .. .it was used as the fuel for miner's lights .. .if you put a drop of water on it produced a flammable gas and miners carbide lights were commonplace .. a favorite of coon hunters also).

Pullet rushed home with his sack of carbide and it was near dark when he got home. He took the sack of carbide out to the hen house and filled all the feeders with it and scattered all the rest on the floor. He went to the house and told the misses that he had found a cheap cure for the ailment that had attacked his chickens. He was so proud of himself.

The next morning after breakfast, Pullet got the egg basket and proudly announced he was going to gather the eggs that his "well" chickens must have laid already. Mrs. Edison was so proud of her smart husband and told him so and gave him a big kiss as he left the house.

Moments later she heard a blood curdling scream from the hen house and she grabbed the shotgun and ran down there. When she opened the door, there stood Pullet in the middle of dead chickens...... every one of them dead as a door nail. Pullet swore" I ort to kill that Jess; that sorry son of a gun"

He grabbed the shotgun from Mrs. Edison, saddled his horse and rode straight to the Claxton place. As he rode up to the house he yelled "Jess, Jess, you chicken doctoring quack- get yore self out here" Jess stuck his head out the door and said "Settle down Pullet, what the dickens is the matter with you?'.

Pullet said "I fed my chickens carbide like you said and every dad blamed one of them died" .

Jess looked at him and said quite innocently "Mine did too".

CHAPTER 25

SEEN US

This was the favorite story of Roger Godwin. I've heard it dozens of times and it was always funny when Roger told it.

This old feller had been quite a rounder. When he died, Saint Peter met him at the pearly gates and said "Old feller, what was the cause of your demise?'" The Old Feller answered "Seen Us"

Saint Peter corrected him by saying" You must mean sinus" "Nope, seen us" replied the Old Feller.

Saint Peter said "I've heard millions of ailments but that is a new one for me - please explain"

The Old Feller said "I was in bed with this other feller's wife - and he seen us"

D. HUNTING STORIES

Believe it or not, from the Civil War era and through the turn of the century and on up until the Second World War, there was much less wild game in Kentucky than there is today. Most of the hunting back in those days was for table meat.

Never the less, hunting prowess and hunting experiences served as the basis of many a tale. Here are just a few of those I remember:

Chapter

26   Squirrel Hunting Scare

27   Bird Hunting During The Great War

28   Slingshot Charlie

29   Fox Hunting

30   Big Bad Bear

Incidentally, I did most of my hunting after I grew up and left Kentucky. Many of my hunting experiences are told in another book, "Bill T's Texas Bob Tales".

CHAPTER 26

SQUIRREL HUNTING SCARE

Marksmanship was always a subject of discussion (and brag) every time a group of hairy legged males gathered around the pot bellied stove in Orange's Store in the winter time.

On this cold, rainy Saturday in December a group of the locals had gathered and the first subject for discussion was shootin. Slim Jones led off by bragging about hitting a 10 point buck deer square between the eyes the past Wednesday morning. He claimed he stepped it off and it was 296 paces from where he was standing when he fired at the big deer.

J.T. "Ace" McGregor said "Heck, that ain't no shootin - big as a deer is and you probably took a rest when you shot". .He then proceeded with his story. said "Last week, forgot which day it was, I was hauling some feed to my steers on the back side of my place. I had just went through the gate of a 40 acre pasture I had to cross to get to the field I had the steers in, and I happened to look across the field to the pond in the far comer and seen two ducks sittin on the pond. I always carry my .22 rifle in the wagon, so, I stopped the team and reached under the seat for the rifle. I figured some roast duck would be some purty good eatin. Anyways, as I was reaching for my gun them ducks must of seen me for they taken off and was flying south. By the time I got the gun to my shoulder I could only see one duck so I led him a little and squeezed off a shot. By cracky, two ducks fell out of the sky. I turned the wagon toward where they fell and giddy upped the team and we went to where the ducks had fell. I counted the steps my off mule taken getting to the dead ducks and near as I recollect it was 1,778 paces."

Slim interrupted" You must have drove around the fence line about 3 times gettin there - and where did you hit the duck, in the guts?'" "Aw naw, shot the eyeballs out of bofum" responded Ace. By now everyone could tell that Slim was getting fed up with Ace's bragging.

Someone got the subject switched to squirrel hunting and Ace allowed that squirrels were mighty scarce this winter. Slim piped up and said" That ain't true, that ridge behind my house with all the pig nut trees on it is just loaded with squirrels". Ace said" That must be where all the squirrels from my place went to then." Slim said" I'm going squirrel hunting in the morning Ace and if you want to come along and demonstrate your shooting skills, be my guest" Ace said "'I'll be at your back door before first light".

It was still dark when Ace rode up to Slim's house on his mule the next morning. Slim had been watching and listening for him and stepped out the house as he rode up. They said their howdies and Slim led his mule to the barn and locked him up, then he returned to the house and got his .22 rifle and said "Let's go kill a mess of squirrels". Ace replied "I'm ready" and breached open his

Fox 12 gauge double barreled shotgun and loaded a couple of shells. Slim hadn't noticed the gun till Ace loaded it and he let out a Hoot and said "Well I be doggone, You aim to hunt squirrels with a blunderbuss quail gun? I sure wish the boys from the store could see this. Every red blooded Kentuckian squirrel hunts with a rifle - not a dad gum scatter gun. And to top it all, you was braggin on what a great shot you are. That was pure D bull crap and I knew it".

Ace mumbled" My rifle was broke so I had to bring my shotgun this morning. Slim continued to mouth off about the shotgun as they walked toward the ridge. As they parted to each go on his way to hunt, Slim said " Ace, I'll bet you a quart of good whiskey that I kill more squirrels this morning with this little bitty .22 than you do with that big ole 12 gauge shotgun. Ace said" Naw, I couldn't take advantage of you like that" and he walked off Ace wandered down the ridge until he found a pig nut tree that the squirrels had been working. The ground was covered with cuttings - nut shells with holes in them where the squirrels had gnawed the meat out of the shell and the sawdust produced in the process. Since Ace was a still hunter, he sat down and leaned back against the tree trunk to await the arrival of the squirrels. The sun rose and it started to warm up a little. Ace reached in his hunting coat pocket, looking for his chewing tobacco. Instead, he found some peanuts he had left in the coat, so he ate a few peanuts. As it got warmer he got more and more comfortable and soon drifted off to sleep.

He awoke with a start! A squirrel was sitting on top of him. (apparently the squirrel was after the peanuts in his pocket). He let out a yell and jumped to his feet. The squirrel took off on the ground as Ace grabbed the shotgun, brought it to his shoulder and shot BLAM! BLAM! The squirrel kept running. While he was reloading, he heard Slim calling him. He answered Slim's call and started walking toward him. As he walked he was trying to think of a good excuse to give for missing the fleeing squirrel.

When he walked up to Slim, Slim was grinning from ear to ear and holding 6 squirrels out in front of himself. Slim inquired" How many did you get?" Ace responded "None to speak of'. Slim said "NONE? I heard two shots. How the heck could you miss with a shotgun?"

Ace said "It's a long story". and Slim quickly responded "Go ahead and tell it - I got all day". Ace said" Well, I know you ain't going to believe this - but it's the Gawd's truth. I sat down by one of them pig nut trees and before I knew it, I fell asleep. Something waken me up. and when I woke up, there was a squirrel crawling up each of my legs, inside of my britches. When they met at my crotch, I heard one of them say to the other - here's two nuts, you want to eat both now or eat one and save the other for supper? Ace had a wild look on his face as he further explained - that shook me up so bad that I jumped up and unzipped my britches and dropped them as I grabbed the gun. They wuz so close when I shot that all that was left of one was his two front teeth and the tip end of his tail is all I could find of the other".

Slim gave him a real skeptical look and Ace said "I told you that you wouldn't believe it".

CHAPTER 27

BIRD HUNTING DURING THE GREAT WAR

All of you readers under fifty don't remember the great war, matter of fact you probably don't even know which was the great war. For my generation, the great war was World War II. It was the last really good war we've had. I was just a kid myself but I remember that war for two reasons mostly, 1. There weren't many young, able bodied men around (they were all in the Army or Navy) and 2. Lots of stuff was scarce (Gas, sugar, tobacco, and especially shotgun shells and bullets)

I had started bird (quail) hunting some with my uncle Arvil before he was drafted into the Army. Before he went off to the big war, he asked me to look after his bird dog till after the war was over and promised we would bird hunt some more when he got back.

His bird dog was a liver spotted pointer named Sissy. She was one of the best bird dogs in the county. Arvil hunted with a 12 gauge Winchester pump shotgun and he was a crack shot. When Sissy pointed a bird and Arvil walked up behind her, you could put the skillet on the fire - there was going to be a dead bird. On the other hand, I hunted with an old hand me down Damascus twist single barrel 12 gauge shotgun. And when Sissy pointed and I was the one walking up behind her, the best bet would be on the bird. I missed - a lot.

When Arvil left, he was about out of shells - and so was I. On the first hunt I took by myself, I used up all the shells. I searched all over the country side for shells, but you couldn't buy any at any price - anywhere. There just weren't any.

One day I was helping a neighbor, Mr. Denny Clark, do some chores around his place. Mr. Clark was crippled and I was helping him on a volunteer basis - didn't know if he was going to pay me or what. Anyway, one of the chores was helping him clean out and straighten out a shed behind his barn. It was full of junk mostly and we threw most of it in the trash. But back in one comer of the shed I uncovered a treasure - a full box of 12 gauge shotgun shells - Peters brand, black powder shells. I placed them on a shelf and wondered if he might give them to me at the end of the day.

When we were finished for the day, Mr. Clark thanked me for helping him and gave me a shiny quarter. Before I went home, I stood around and finally got up enough nerve to ask him "How much would you take for that box of shotgun shells?" He thought for a minute and responded "They ought to be worth at least a dollar I expect". I was completely dejected; I had thought he would take the hint and sell them to me for the quarter. Anyway, I didn't give up and told him "I want them shells real bad but all the

money I got is a quarter - could I pay you 25 cents now and the rest later?'. He smiled and patted me on the head as he said "Aw heck, the shells are so old they probably won't even shoot - they are even black powder shells - Keep your quarter and I'll give you the shells". I was thrilled and got the shells and started planning a bird hunt as I walked home.

Saturday morning, bright and early, I was knocking on Aunt Ouida's (Arvil's wife) back door and when she answered I asked if she wanted some quail for supper. She said "Sure, where you gonna get any quail?'. I told her of my good fortune with Mr. Clark and that I could now go shoot some birds with the shells I had acquired.

She said" Let me pack you a lunch and put some scraps in for Sissy. You will get hungry if you stay long". She knew that Arvil would hunt from daylight till dark and figured I was from the same bolt of cloth.. While she fixed the lunch I went to the dog pen and loved on Sissy and turned her out. She was so excited at the thought of going hunting - so was I. I planned on taking a big circle back toward Copeland's Bluff, that way I would hunt mostly on property owned by relatives. (but I could have hunted on most any neighbors property just as well).

There was a bumper crop of birds that year, they were all over the place. We hadn't gone more than 200 yards from the house before Sis started acting "birdie". She started trailing birds and I hurried up so I could keep her in sight. Soon she was on point and the adrenalin was really flowing as I walked up behind her - then WHIRR! and I was startled as the covey took to the air. (I don't care how many birds you have flushed or how long you have bird hunted - that first covey rise always startles you) Instinctively, I cocked the hammer on the old single shot, threw it to my shoulder, and fired KA BLAM! I was immediately engulfed in a cloud of black smoke and could not see a thing. I had no idea if I had hit anything. Those old black powder sheets sure created some smoke.

In a minute, the smoke had dissipated and I saw Sis out in the weeds ahead of me, her tail was wagging frantically as she trailed something. As I was reloading, she pointed again. I figured it was a cripple so I said "Dead bird - fetch" She moved and the bird took off but she leaped and literally caught it in the air and brought it to me. I popped its head and examined it before I put it in my coat pocket. I could feel a couple of pellets that had just barely broken the skin. Those old shells didn't pack much punch - just

smoke.

I started to walk in the direction I thought the covey had flown but Sissy went right back to the spot where she had caught the bird and started trailing another one. I figured it must be a cripple (probably a broken wing) so I just stood and watched her for a minute and she came to another point. I said "Dead bird - fetch" again and she stepped forward and caught the bird and brought it to me. Again, I popped its head and examined it also - as I suspected, it had a broken wing but I couldn't locate any other pellets in it. I petted Sissy and rubbed her head and bragged on her a minute before moving on. I was feeling right proud of myself too - two birds and just one shot. At this rate we would have a whole sack full of birds before lunch time.

In a few minutes she started acting birdie again and was soon on point. I walked up behind her and a single bird came up and I instinctively fired at it. The smoke screen created by this shell was even worse than the first shot had been. By the time the smoke had cleared enough that I could see, Sissy was back at my feet with a dead bird in her mouth. I petted her and bragged on her some more as I took the bird from her. As I started to pop the head of this bird, I felt a pellet in its head. This had been a clean kill ..

But that was the last bird I sacked up on this hunt. After we crossed the bottoms we moved up into the hills and the birds were much wilder up there. Even though Sissy worked hard, she also worked carefully. But no use, many of the birds were flushing ahead of her. I must have wasted 10 shots at these birds that were almost out of range for good shells even. Then we jumped a red fox and I wasted another 4 shells on it. But that explained why the birds were so wild, the fox had been after them.

When we got to the base of Copeland's Bluff, I decided it was time for a lunch break so we stopped by a spring. We each got a long drink of water and I sat down and opened the lunch sack and fed Sis her scraps then ate my sandwich and apple. We both lay down and took a little nap. After we had rested up good we started back.

The birds we had flushed that morning were scattered everywhere and it seemed that Sis was constantly on point and often I would flush a bird as I walked to her. I shot so many times that it seemed the whole country side was one gigantic smoke screen. By the time we reached the bottoms, I was completely out of shells so I had Sis heel and we walked on toward the house. She was looking at me with an expression that said "That sure was fun, but heck fire, you're a lousy shot".

I sure wished that I had a decent gun and some good live ammunition so I could have proved to her that it was the war that caused the problem, not my shooting ability.

(After the great war was over and Arvil returned, I was able to trade for a neat little 20 gauge double and shells became available again and we took many a great hunt).

CHAPTER 28

SLINGSHOT CHARLIE

I don't know at the number of Slingshot Charlie stories I've heard over the years. I've heard stories originating in Tennessee, Missouri, Georgia, Alabama, etc. Old Charlie must have moved around a lot or there was more than one of him. Anyway, this story was told by Granddad about a Slingshot Charlie who lived near the Macedonia school.

Charlie had been shooting a slingshot since he was five years old. He had become very proficient with a slingshot and used it to hunt small game.

One day Charlie's cousin (second cousin I think) came down from Hopkinsville to go squirrel hunting. He brought a 12 gauge shotgun to hunt with. His name was Sam Newman.

When Sam arrived at the Newman farm, Charlie was out at the barn milking. Sam went on down to the barn and visited with Charlie for a minute and asked him if he wanted to go squirrel hunting with him. Charlie said" I would, except I got to finish my chores" So Sam pitched in and helped finish milking, feeding the horses, slopping the hogs, and even left a bucket of shelled com by the hen house so Ma Newman wouldn't have to go all the way to the com crib after it.

Now they could go hunting. Sam got his shotgun and stuffed his pockets with shotgun shells. Charlie went in the house and got a pocket full of marbles and his slingshot which he put in his hip pocket. He joined Sam and they headed toward the creek bottoms. They had gone a ways when Sam realized that Charlie wasn't carrying a gun. Sam asked "Charlie, ain't you goin to hunt?'" "Yep" was Charlie's reply. "But you ain't carrying a gun" exclaimed Sam. "Yep" again responded Charlie and kept walking ..

When they come to the edge of the timber, they split up and agreed to stay close enough to one another to hear each other whistle. Sam was afraid he would get lost.   After they had gone about 200 yards, Charlie heard Sam blasting away BLAM! BLAM! then BLAM! BLAM! (Sam was using a double barrel).

They continued deeper into the woods, now and then one or the other would whistle, and Charlie heard Sam blast away several more times. They came to the fence and Charlie signaled for Sam to turn around and head back in the direction they had come from. About three hours later Sam emerged from the woods and started whistling for Charlie. Charlie finally whistled back and directly stepped out of the woods about 50 yards away and walked down to where Sam was at.

When Charlie walked up, Sam pulled two badly shot up squirrels out of his pocket and proudly displayed them for Charlie to inspect. Charlie's comment was " Them is shot up purty bad, ain't much meat left fit to eat on em". Charlie was a little upset by that remark and asked" Where's ery squirrel you kilt?" Charlie reached around his belt and removed six grey squirrels and one big red fox squirrel and threw them on the ground. As he did, his slingshot fell out of his pocket.

Sam's eyes popped out and he exclaimed "Gee cousin Charlie, you had real good luck didn't you?" "Naw" replied Charlie, " I had to shoot twice at that big fox squirrel"

CHAPTER 29

FOX HUNTING

Most West Kentucky farms had a pack of dogs back in the good old days. Some had coon hounds and some had fox hounds - but hounds never the less. The fundamental difference between coon hunters and fox hunters was that coon hunters killed the coons and saved their hides to sell whereas fox hunters got their pleasure out of hearing the hounds run. Matter of fact, they would get real angry at anyone who filled a fox - especially if the fox was killed in front of the dogs.

My granddad Lib Thomas was a coon hound man and thought fox hunters were silly and fox hunting was a waste of time. He was the local magistrate and had once fined one of the local fox hunters $20 for allowing his fox hound female dog to be bred by one of his stud coon hounds. And if the fox hunters ever ran a fox across his farm, Granddad would always try to shoot the fox. So you can see, Granddad was not popular with the fox hunting crowd.

One of the fox hunters was a friend of my dad and he stopped by our place one day and asked if they could hunt on our property. I was there when he asked so I asked if could go fox hunting with them. He couldn't say no in front of dad so he said "Sure" followed by Dad saying "Sure" also. That night the fox hunters gathered at our place and turned the hounds loose and we struck out in a westerly direction toward the Mount Pisgah Baptist Church. There were six (including me) hunters and fifteen hounds. Each hunter could recognize the bark and cry of each of his hounds and could tell what each hound was doing by the sounds. Each hound had a name and it seemed that part of the sport was bragging on your hound(s).

The pack of hounds on this particular night consisted of Bugle Ann, Bull Throat, Rowdy, all owned by Joy Cox; Tenderfoot and Rustler owned by Pullet Edison; Rusty, Spot, and Lulu, owned by Mo Tucker; Liberty Bell, Constitution, and Antioch, owned by Oscar Rush (a teacher); and finally J.T. Boyd and his prized hounds, Lightning, Thunder, Rain Dance, and Sophie Tucker. And me of course. Mr. Cox introduced me to all the hunters - it seemed like he was sort of in charge of the hunt.

After we climbed our west fence and got on Joe Toliver's property Mr. Cox ordered us to stop. "Listen, he ordered". We all listened and soon off to the south and west we could hear "yo, yo, yo, yooooo" then an occasional chopped up "yow, yow". Mr. Cox said" Bull Throat has hit a cold trail and old Thunder has joined him. About that time we an excited "yowll!" and Mr. Cox continued " That sounds like Liberty Bell and darn if I don't believe she has jumped that fox and we are about to have us a real race. If it's the same old fox we've run before he's mighty sly and it will be a challenge to keep him moving. Let's move further west and get up on that bluff so we can hear better. In the past, that fox has made a big circle and come back this way and the hounds always loose him near the railroad trestle over Montgomery Creek.

We got to the bluff and climbed up on top of it and built a big fire and gathered round to hear the hounds make sweet hound dog music. By then that was the darndest conglomeration of hound voices you ever heard - hunters too. Every time you heard a different sound from the hounds, one of the hunters would speak up "There's old Antioch", "Lulu has moved to the lead". "Rain Cloud is really crowding him, sounds like he is running by sight now". And Mr. Cox was giving a running commentary of the race"
They're going across Jim Ed's com field now - now they are going behind Turkey Mountain (notice how the sound is fading, that's cause they are behind the mountain, etc,"

Finally, we quit hearing the hounds. There were all sorts of theories as to what had happened. "That old fox went to ground (went in a hole)" or "That there run like a grey fox and he probably climbed a tree" or "That's that cagy old fox we run some last year and he swum the river on em" etc. Nobody could agree, it was all speculation. Finally, J. T. pulled out a pint of whiskey from his coat pocket and took a big swig before he offered his guess. He said" Fellers, I bet I know what happened. The last time we heard them hounds they were about to cross over on to Lib Thomas's place. I'll bet you a dollar to a hole in a doughnut that old rascal heard them coming and slipped out and killed the fox."

When he said that, there was finally some agreement among the fraternity. They all started mouthing off about how bad "that old Lib" was. Each had a incident to describe to illustrate his meanness. Finally, Mr. Cox, who had not been able to get a word in edgewise, stood up and looked over the bunch and said, "Boys, you must not of been paying attention when I introduced our guest, young Mr. Thomas here. This is Lib's grandson.

It really got quiet around the fire. Pullet finally got up and went over and picked up a sack he had been carrying and produced a gallon of white lightning (moonshine).

He took a big gulp from the jug and passed it around the fire. When the jug made it back to Pullet, he took another gulp and said "You know, old Lib ain't too bad a feller- He loaned me a disc once when I broke mine - here Mo, take another drink; Mo took a big swallow and said" Member that time I was charged with stealing some seed com and was put before Magistrate Lib ..... Well, he rode up to Oranges store and when he found out I had bought some seed com there that spring - he ruled I wasn't guilty - and I wasn't" here J.T., your turn, and J.T. took a long slug of the moonshine and said "Heck, I member when Lib used to teach Sunday school at the church, he's a fine feller"

They even let me have just a taste of that white lightning and I relaxed around the fire with them as they converted my Granddad from a terrible sinner to a saint.

CHAPTER 30

BIG BAD BEAR

Uncle Josh White told this story about an encounter he had with a big bear back in the days of his youth. He was sixteen when this happened.

It was winter time and the family was low on meat. It was even lower on money. His rifle was broken but he didn't have the money to get it fixed. He was wondering what to do. He needed to kill a deer for table meat but deer were getting few and far between. He thought about making a bow and arrow but knew he probably could never get close enough for a kill with that kind of a weapon.

His mother had noticed that Josh was thinking hard on something and asked "Joshua - what's trouble you?".

Josh said "Maw, this family needs some red meat to eat and my gun is broke - I can't go kill us a deer." Maw said "Why don't you use your pa's old gun - it's hanging over the fireplace". (His pa was killed in a sawmill accident when Josh was 11 years old and Josh took over as family provider for his mother and seven brothers and sisters at that time). Josh said "That's an idea - I'll try it".

He went to the fireplace and took down the old Kentucky .50 caliber muzzle loader, oiled, and examined it. It was loaded - good thing because he had no powder, rifle balls, or caps - he would have to kill a deer with his one and only shot.

Later in the day it started snowing and Josh decided he would wait until the next morning to go hunting. Deer were scarce but he had seen a doe in the Montgomery Creek bottoms a couple of weeks ago and figured he could locate her tracks in the snow and track her down and get close enough for a good shot.

Before daylight the next morning he got up and dressed in his warmest clothes, put on his boots, got the Kentucky rifle, and headed for the bottoms. Soon it was daylight and just as he figured, he cut the tracks of two deer down by Montgomery Creek - a doe and a smaller deer - probably her fawn. He started tracking them up the creek bank. After about a half mile of tracking the tracks indicated the deer had started to run. Not good he thought. He figured he had got too close and spooked them. Well, nothing to do but stay on their trail.

In about a hundred yards Josh discovered what really frightened the deer. Big bear tracks came in from an angle and followed the deer tracks. Josh thought - maybe Lem Potts was right. Lem has claimed a big bear had raided his hog pen a couple of weeks ago and killed and ate one of his shoats. No one had believed him because no bears had been seen in this part of the country in years. Maybe this bear had wandered up from East Tennessee.

It made no difference how the bear got there - there was no doubt he was now following bear tracks and it frightened him a little. He knew his departed father had killed bear with the Kentucky rifle but he didn't know if one shot would get the job done. He would prefer the deer for - table meat but had heard the old folks tell how good bear meat was to eat - so if he had to shoot a bear - he would still have red meat for supper.

The tracks soon led into a really thick and tangled thicket. He hesitated before following the thick brush but proceeded slowly and cautiously. When he got deep into the thickest there was a terrible "Grawl" and a thrashing in the bushes as the big bear pounced on him from behind and wrapped his strong front legs around him. He smelled its terrible breath and Saliva dripped from its jaws. He could not use his arms to reach his knife nor get loose to pick up the Kentucky rifle which he had dropped.

What was he going to do to escape the clutches of this big bad powerful bear. He suddenly remembered a story he had heard once abut Davy Crockett, a Tennessee mountain man, who had faced this exact problem. He thought "What have I got to lose "As he carefully worked his right hand behind him and felt until he found the big bad bears thing. He gently wrapped his fingers around it and started pumping - slowly at first then more rapidly. In no time the bear started relaxing his hold on him and finally Josh was able to pull away and start fighting his way out of the thicket to a large corn field on the other side. When he broke out of the thicket into the field he ran as fast and as far as he could.

When he had crossed the field he was completely out of breath so he stopped to regain it. He glanced back to see if the bear was following. No - No bear.

As soon as he got his wind back he straightened up and again looked across the field at the thicket from which he escaped. The big bad bear emerged from the thicket, stood up on its hind legs and looked across the field and started waving his front legs (arms) in a "come back" motion.

Note - Uncle Josh never told this story until he was past 50 years old.

E. STORIES CLOSE TO HOME

Now, we're getting down to the nitty gritty of this story telling. The stories are too close to home for comfort so I have darn sure changed the names of the characters. (Note to relatives - if you recognize yourself - don't tell and I won't).

Here are the stories I've put in this category:

Chapter

31 Good Bourbon And Bad Moonshine

32 Mind Your Table Manners

33 Maine

34 Can't Find My Fistes

35 Tobacco Crop Money

36 Chawin Tebaccer

37 Uncle Bob's Flying Machine

38 Spooks and Goblins

39 Uncle Dewey's Motor Sickle

CHAPTER 31

GOOD BOURBON AND BAD MOONSHINE

Kentucky is noted for its beautiful horses, fast women, burley tobacco, and fine bourbon whiskey--all of which can be downright habit forming.

For you folks who purchase and consume bourbon, let me assure you that it is fine stuff made in the big distilleries around the L's--Louisville, Lexington, and Lawrenceburg. I can testify that it's good for you and helps you too, besides all the benefit you get out of it. I personally have drunk enough of it to float a battleship in it--and it --ain't hurt me none. Shucks! I don't have to tell you though; you can tell that from this literature I'm composing.

The bourbon whiskey (Why do they spell whiskey--w-h-i-s-k-y--on a Scotch bottle?) which I'm remembering is the kind which was made in a "still" from family recipes (utilizing mostly <u>corn</u> for the mash) back up the heads of hundreds of hollows in the State. I've helped my granddad make a few batches of the wonderful juice which is known as "moonshine ," "white lightning," "Kickapoo joy juice," "panther pee," and dozens of other descriptive names.

Basically, it's all the same--homemade corn whiskey--and borders on nitroglycerin and strychnine. I've heard tales of how good old man Smith's whiskey (from near Goldenpond) was or old man Jones' whiskey (from up around Mannington), etc., etc. Wal, I've tried about all of it; and, I'm here to tell you--it ain't fit to drink. However, if it's the results that you're interested in--that's another matter.

Homemade corn whiskey will probably make you drunker quicker and sounder than any potent ever-devised by mortal man. After a couple of swallers, you won't know whose boy you are; and after another one you won't give a darn.

I remember that my great-granddad used to tell this story about he and his cousin, Shretly Smiley, making a big batch of squeezins one day; and as the first run came off the still and dripped into the fruit jar, he said, Shretly, we've been working hard gettin' this batch made, why don't we have a little snort; it is almost sundown anyway. Shretly said, "Naw, I don't like it raw like this. Let's let 'er age some and have a drink about dark."

My granddad also liked to tell about the time a peddler stopped by the farm selling his wares--axes, knives, etc.; and, he was offered a drink of white lightning--which he graciously refused. Uncle Mort took offense and pulled the old double-barreled Wheeler shotgun off the pegs, placed the barrels right up to the peddler's ear, and said, "It ain't polite to refuse a drink of homemade likker in these parts--now drink." The peddler rolled his eyes around at Uncle Mort, tilted the jug way back, and took two or three powerful swallows of the juice. When he let the jug back down, steam was coming out of his ears and nose; and his hair had commenced to stand straight up!

Uncle Mort relaxed the gun from his head--looked him square in the eye and said, "That was a right social swig you took, stranger--now, hold the gun on me so I can take a big swaller."

There weren't many accommodations for "outsiders" in West Kentucky in the good old days. Most everyone lived on his own place, and towns were few and far between. The most "famous" eatin' and drinkin' place was Orvil Craynor's Cafe on the Dawson-Kuttawa Road.

Orvil had the reputation of being the best moonshiner in West Kentucky. His whiskey which he made back in the hills and sold at his cafe was some good-real true sippin' whiskey.

However, the food was neglected because most all the natives came there for the drinkin' anyway.

A favorite story around the cafe involved the old burly logger, Charles Sisk, who came in on Saturday night and ordered a jug of whiskey, a steak, and a hound dawg. Orvil asked him "Charles, why in the heck do you want a hound dawg?"

Charles replied, "To eat the darn lousy steak which you fix!"

And, of course, everyone in Kentucky has heard this one; but I'll repeat it for you foreigners who might be reading this treasury of Kentucky 'folklore!

Lightnin' Smith was plowing his cornpatch by the road one day, and his neighbor drove by and stopped to "chew the cud" awhile. Finally, the neighbor commented on how good the corn crop was looking; he asked, ""What do you figger it'll produce this year-?" Lightnin' replied, "Wal, if we get a good rain in late June or early July, I figger she'll make at least ten gallons to the acre this year."

CHAPTER 32

MIND YOUR TABLE MANNERS

Generally, the country folk raised most everything that they ate. It's a good thing--they didn't have money to buy anything! Most of the items which were store bought were really store bartered. The farmer traded a can of cream or a basket of eggs to the merchant for the staples which he needed --sugar, salt, coffee, tobacco, shells (ammunition), etc.

However, before you start feeling sorry for them, consider the fact that they probably ate better than you! They butchered their own beef, pork, and poultry-- caught fish, killed and trapped wild game; and the garden vegetables were abundant and varied (corn, beans, beets, cucumbers, squash, melons, tomatoes, peppers, onions, potatoes: etc.). And, nearly every farm had fruit trees (apple, pear, cherry, plums, etc.) The surplus was canned in Mason jars and stored in the cellar for the winter months. Milk, eggs, and butter were from the cows and chickens (which were a necessity on any farm) .

Abundant Times

Many's the time when I have sat down to my grandmother's table when it would contain three or four meat dishes (fried chicken, beef short ribs, ham, etc.), six or eight vegetables, cornbread and biscuits, a pie and cake, sweet milk and buttermilk, butter, and various jams and jellies. My grandmother would flutter around the kitchen and then come to the table after everyone was seated and would probably say:

1. "Take out to the bread and meat--if you see anything fittin' to eat."

or

2. "I'm sorry that I didn't have any lite bread to serve with the cornbread and biscuits."

or

3. "There's plenty more on the stove when you run out. " (There would be enough on the table already for a small army.)

Lean Times

There were lean times too. Particularly in late winter when we would start running low on canned goods and cured meat. The cows and chickens weren't too cooperative about then either cause there wasn't a goodly supply of feed for them.

Usually, the corn held up pretty good; and when all else was running low or out, you could haul a load of corn to the mill, have it ground into meal; and take the last silver dollar in the sugar bowl in the top shelf of the cupboard and buy a sack of soup (great northern) beans.

It was during such a period when we had been on an extended soup bean and corn bread diet when good fortune struck. Mr. Ed Simons, the postman, got pneumonia and dad got to substitute carry his mail route for a week for $5 U. S.

cash money. He got carried away with his good fortune, blew about $2 of it on groceries, and brought them home. He had flour, sugar, coffee, more soup beans, a can of syrup, and even a sack of horehound candy.

That night we really celebrated, and mom whipped up a batch of biscuits for supper to go with the corn bread and soup beans. The youngest, Calvin, said after he had filled his plate with hot biscuits, "Mammy, will you hand me some bread (meaning corn bread) to go with my biscuits?"

CHAPTER 33

MAINE

I have knocked around the country quite a bit the last several years since leaving my beloved Pennyrile area of Kentucky. One thing I have noted is that folks are basically the same the world over. Or, as one of my professors in the school of hard knocks once put it--"people are just people."

In striking up acquaintances wherever I've gone in this world (I suspect it would be the same if I went to Mars, the moon, or some such.), the three basics that everybody tries to drag out of you are 1. What's your name? 2. What do you do? and 3. Where are you from?

My replies have been 1. Just plain ole Bill Thomas (except in certain instances when a pseudonym seemed advisable). 2. I'm a bookkeeper* and 3. Maine. The third answer always brings forth a question something like this -- "Maine, hmm, darn Yankee, I ain't never met anyone from Maine before-- what part of Maine are you from?" My reply: The main part of the world <u>West Kentucky</u>." (Actually, I'm from Dawson Springs, Kentucky--that's near Piney Grove, Beulah, St. Charles, Nortonville, Crossroads., Charleston, Mortons Gap, and all those other big West Kentucky metropolitan areas that you all have been reading about.)

This book contains some of' the stories of that part of the woods that I remember from the good old days. (The good old days for everyone are simply-- the days of their youth.)

*I hesitate to say C.P.A. or accountant - most folks to this day still don't understand these terms.

CHAPTER 34

CAN'T FIND MY FISTES

Social life in the country was limited--except for church on Sunday, a graveyard cleaning or two during the summer, and an occasional house- or barn-raising, there wasn't much else to do. However, when there was a party, everybody tried to catch up; and it about made up for it--they were real humdingers.

Most parties were about the same (that is, all three or four I heard about). They were attended by the folks around the country of "courtin" age. Generally, they were at some of the girls' houses; and that night her family would clear out and leave the young folk to their carrying-ons.

For a day or two the girls would make cakes, candy, popcorn balls, candy apples, and other goodies for the party. For liquid refreshments the usual bill of fare was apple cider--provided by the girls, that is. Some of the boys always brought a jug or two of "white lightning" and kept it hid out in their buggy or wagon. This liquid always caused "trouble" before the party was over.

Generally, when the party was gittin' started and the crowd was gathering, things were right formal and most everyone was ill at ease--particularly, if there was a stranger or two in the crowd and if there was a disproportion of the sexes--which there usually was--about ten or twelve boys for eight or ten girls.

However, after it got good and dark, they had played a few parlor games, bobbed an apple or two, and the young men had slipped out and nipped at the jug a time or two--the party would liven up. Before you knew it, there would be a game or two of "spin the bottle" going on. (For you uninformed, spin the bottle was played by boys and girls forming a circle with a bottle lying flat on the floor in the center. In turn, each player would give the bottle a spin; and when it stopped, the person of the opposite whom it was pointing toward became the winner of a kiss from the spinner. Most everyone was bashful, and the "pair" would skip down the hall to the kitchen or bedroom for the "kiss." This little game could also create problems--particularly, if two or three of the "couples" at the party were going steady-like.

At this party held at the Cranor place in the fall of the year, there was in attendance Slim Nichols and his galfriend, Bessie Lowe. Slim was known to have a purty short fuse and had exploded a time or two in the past.

Bessie Lowe had already created quite a commotion and gotten Slim riled up when she came into the living room shouting, "I've been geesed." Slim said, "You mean goosed?" Bessie Lou said, "Do you think I'm stupid or something--I can tell when they use two fingers."

The Croft boys brought their cousin from Cadiz with them. His name was Calvin Croft, and he was a big, old, raw-boned, gawky kid but kind of likeable. The Croft boys were always playing pranks, and they saw an excellent chance to have some fun that night with old Calvin. They got a big kick out of introducing Calvin as kind of clumsy--so clumsy he couldn't hit a bull in the butt with a bass fiddle. Calvin was good-natured about it and would join in the laughter himself.

Calvin didn't join in any of the games--being a stranger--and a mighty bashful one at that. As the night wore on and the party got rowdier and rowdier, Calvin was beginning to get into the spirit of things--particularly, after the Croft boys had gotten him out at the buggy and poured some liquid spirits down him.

One of the girls who had taken a shine to Calvin came over and asked him to join their game which they were starting; and his resistance had dropped to zero, so he accepted. The game turned out to be another "spin the bottle" session. Included in the circle were Slim Nichols and Bessie Lowe.

Calvin was elected to spin first, and as the luck of the spin would have it-- Calvin spun the bottle and when it stopped--it was pointing square dab at Bessie Lowe. Calvin, by now, wasn't too bashful; so he walked across the Circle, grabbed Bessie, and gave her a big, sloppy kiss right in front of everybody. Slim's fuse started burning when the bottle stopped and hit powder when the lips met. He let out a cuss word or two, jumped on poor Calvin, and started pounding him with roundhouse rights and lefts.

With the commotion and racket, everybody crowded into the room to witness the fight--which was considerably one-sided since Calvin hadn't gotten in a lick.

When the Croft boys got into the room and saw what was going, one of them yelled, "Hit him, Calvin, hit him hard!" Calvin grunted as he caught another right in the belly and said, "I can't." The Croft boy asked, "Why?"

Calvin said in an embarrassed sort of way, "I can't find my fistes."

CHAPTER 35

TOBACCO CROP MONEY

All of the stories up to now have come from my paternal side of the family, who were for the most part fun-loving, hill country farmers, but poor. This story comes from my maternal side of the family, who were flatland, Scotchmen farmers.

My maternal Great-granddad, W. J. Simmons, was a tobacco farmer who had a blackland farm in Trigg County. He was Scotch through and through and was so tight he squeaked when he walked. I would be agreeable to make a large wager that he had the first nickel he ever made tucked in his pocket the day he expired. I have heard him tell this tale many times --which, I believe, is true.

Back in the late 1800's the only money crop grown by the farmers in Trigg County to speak of was the tobacco crop. (Sometimes, the corn crop was also a money crop if properly converted to a liquid and marketed carefully--but this was not to speak of.)

According to W. J., the drought in 1898 almost wiped him out. The tobacco was awful small and scrawny and never did fully mature. However, after he had put almost a full year of labor into the crop, he decided to take it to market anyway--even if it didn't bring two bits.

If you ever messed around with a tobacco crop before the days of modern technology, you could better understand his attitude. In those days it was about a year-round job to raise a tobacco crop. You started in the winter by clearing out a plot in the woods for a plant bed. The timber and brush were stacked in the cleared plot and burned--the ashes contained a lot of potash, which was just what the seed needed to make a healthy "set" (plant). After the last freeze the seeds were planted and the bed covered with cheesecloth.

In the spring, after you had your tobacco patch laid by and furrowed (all done with a team of horses or mules), you then had to transplant the sets from the plant bed to the tobacco patch.

While the young plants were growing, you had to cultivate them to keep the weeds out and soil broken so it could absorb oxygen, etc., from the air. Then the plants got taller, the cultivating was done with a hoe--also, any thinning. Throughout the growth, you also had to constantly keep the tobacco worms pulled off the plants and stomped. Some of those vile-looking worms got so big that you had to stomp them two or three times to kill them.

After the plants reached semimaturity, a second leaf would start to bud out just over the existing leaf--these had to be nipped out by hand in a process called "suckering." (I think that term applied to the darn fool doing the nipping.) As the plants got nearer to maturity, the top of the plant was cut-off in another process called topping.

If you think a burning cigarette makes a mess lying in a clear glass ashtray, you should see a live human being emerge from a tobacco patch after a day of "suckering!! tobacco!! in mid-July. There ain't many sights of a more raunchy and grimy-looking mortal~ And, if you think we are through "raising tobacco" at this point, think again. You now have to harvest the crop.

Harvesting consisted of first getting the crop from the field to the barn. This was done by cutting each stalk at ground level with a tobacco knife (machete type of knife), spiking it on a tobacco stick (about 5 or 6 stalks per stick), and then stacking it gently on a mule-drawn sled. It was then hauled to the tobacco barn where it was "racked" to the rafters. When the barn was full, a hickory-fire was built in it to "cure" the tobacco --this process took days in itself.

On the rainy days after the tobacco was cured, it was taken down and stripped--that is, each individual leaf was pulled from the stalk and several wrapped together in a package called a "hand". The "hands" were then packed in a barrel called a "hogshead"--and that's how it went to market. The stalks were hauled back and scattered on the field for fertilizer.

Anyway, the reason I gave you all this background on raising tobacco is you can appreciate the rest of this story.

W. J. had spent the better part of the year fooling with his scrawny crop of tobacco when word came that the tobacco sale would be held at the Hopkinsville tobacco auction the first week of December. The last few days of November he and his sons loaded up three wagonloads of tobacco hogsheads, and he packed up a toe sack with essentials (some hardtack, sowbelly, jerky, salt, an old pistol, and matches), a couple of quilts, tarp, jug of water, and grain and hay for the oxen.

On November 29 he hitched up six braces of oxen to the wagons and headed out to Hopkinsville. It was a cold and rainy day; and W. C. didn't particularly look forward to the two-day ride with those slow-plodding oxen--but, after all the hard work that went into the crop, you couldn't have stopped him from making the trip if you had to.

He made purty fair time that first day even though the roads were muddy and slick and the oxen were pulling hard. Late that afternoon a "blue norther" came roaring through, and the roads started to freeze up. By dark they were traveling at a right fast clip--for oxen anyway. He drove on for 'out an hour after dark to a holler which was at about the halfway point and which he knew had a good camping spot: cave, spring, and plenty of firewood.

He pulled the wagons off the main road into a log road that ran up into the holler, drove them up to a point below the cave, and left them hitched while he climbed up to the cave with an armload of sticks and leaves which he had gathered in the darkness. At the cave entrance he piled them up, struck a match, and lit the leaves--in their light he scrounged around for more twigs and leaves and added them to the fire. Soon, he had a nice fire going and put a few larger limbs and logs on it from the pile of wood which a previous "traveler" had left by the cave entrance, as was the custom.

When he had thawed out and warmed up a bit by the fire, he climbed back down to the wagon, unhitched the oxen, and fed and watered them in the makeshift pen made from logs. Having the teams taken care of for the night, he got his sack of essentials, filled his jug at the spring, and climbed back up the cave to fix his supper and get settled in for the night.

The fire had died down some, and he had a bed of hot embers which was just right for cooking. The smoke had cleared out of the cave; and it was nice and warm--much like a stove oven after bread was baked and removed, he thought.

W. J. made supper off of some pieces of sowbelly, which he cooked on a stick over the fire, and some cold biscuits which his wife had thoughtfully wrapped in a cloth and slipped into his sack. He smiled at her thoughtfulness.

After the meal he raked up a pile of leaves inside the cave, placed his tarpaulin and quilts over the leaves, and settled in for a much-deserved rest. He fell asleep immediately; and the owl hoots and wolf howls didn't bother him a bit--he was used to those sounds but more--he was beat.

At daybreak he awoke, pulled on his boots, got up, stirred up the coals, and built up the fire. He then went down to feed and water the oxen again and check on the wagons.

By now, the woods had come alive as the birds began to sing;- the squirrels came out of their dens and started to scurry about. One young squirrel came down to the pen where the oxen were and started to eat some of the grain which was on the ground--when W. J. noticed the squirrel, he decided that he might make a quick change on the breakfast menu! He picked up three or four good-sized rocks, slipped very quietly to the pen, and climbed up on the fence. He was in luck--the squirrel hadn't left his breakfast of grain. W. J. decided to try a "shot.gun" throw; so he drew back and threw all the rocks at once at the squirrel--and his luck held--one of the rocks hit the squirrel (now breakfast) right square in the head. He picked up the squirrel, cleaned him in a wink, cut a forked stick, and skewered him. He took him back to the cave, put some salt on him, rubbed him good with sowbelly, and stuck the stick in the ground so that the squirrel would cook slowly and tenderly over the coals. While the squirrel was cooking, he made a pot of tea, packed up his quilts and tarpaulin, and hitched up the oxen to the wagons. He then went off into the woods, did his morning ritual, and came back to the spring and washed up.

By this time, the squirrel was cooked just right; and he ate most of it for breakfast--washed down with hot tea. He saved a couple of pieces of squirrel meat for lunch and carefully wrapped them in the cloth with the· two remaining biscuits. He carried some wood up to the woodpile to replenish what he had used and kicked dirt over the fire to put it out.

He climbed down to the wagons hitched up the oxen, got his "bull whip"--cracked it once, let out a stream of his favorite oxen commands (which contained some choice cuss words), and they moved out toward the main road.

It was very cold that morning; and W. J. hoped it would stay that way --the roads were frozen solid and they were making good time. He kept urging the teams on. The sun peeped out for awhile; but at W.J.'s urging, it finally ducked back in behind some clouds--and stayed there.

They passed several farms and W. J. knew most of the farmers but he didn't slow down. He would wave or yell if anyone came out, and a couple of the farmers trotted down to the road and walked along with him for a mile or two to catch up on the news from Trigg County and pass on any news which they knew. Also, a few mean-looking hound dogs would come tearing down the fields and come running up like they were going to eat both him and the oxen up; but a crack of the bull whip over their heads or on their flanks sent them yelping back to whence they came.

All in all, it was an uneventful day; and he came into sight of Hopkinsville about three o'clock that afternoon. By four-thirty he was at the tobacco barns and had his oxen unhitched, fed, and penned for the night.

They had some improvised "bunks" over in the corner of one of the barns and an old pot-bellied stove there. There was a huge. pot of coffee on top of the stove, and W. J. took his sack of essentials and quilts and headed for the "quarters." Several of the tobacco farmers had already arrived and "staked out" their beds. W. J. walked up and renewed old acquaintances as well as met two or three men he didn't know over a cup of hot coffee. He casually selected his bed and placed his gear on it. W. J. always looked

toward these tobacco sales with mixed emotions. He really enjoyed the fellowship of his comrades in tobacco farming and loved to sit around as a bystander and watch them gamble at cards, drag on jugs, and tell boisterous stories. However, he hated like the devil to go to the boarding house and spend his hard earned money on food. He knew if he didn't join them they would really "hurrah" him for being so tight he wouldn't eat. They ribbed him plenty for not gambling or joining them in drink--but, there were several others who didn't participate; so there was some relief on that score. But--all of them ate at the boarding house and he had no choice there. He reluctantly parted with 15 to 20¢ each tobacco sale for food even though it hurt him through and through!

W. J. had been to tobacco sales many times, and he was wise in the ways of the tobacco farmers. He knew they would have a lantern near the stove, and that several of them would stay up most of the night gambling and drinking. He, therefore, picked a pile of hay in the far corner--the furthest from the fire--for his bed. Early that night he slipped from the crowd around the fire, picked his way through the semi-darkness to his bed, crawled into it, and pulled the quilts over his head. He soon got accustomed to the sound the carryings-on near the fire and went to sleep. He awoke early the next morning and took advantage of his early rising. Instead of going to the fire and drinking coffee before heading for breakfast, he slipped out and got his team of oxen, hitched them to his wagon, and put it at the head of the line; he then moved the next two in line behind it. When this was completed, a couple of other "old heads" were up and about and started moving their wagons in line behind his. W. J. also knew that his tobacco was not a good grade; but he figured that if it was sold first, it might bring a better price since the prices of each sale were posted and a low, early price might have a bad effect on the farmers.

W. J. decided to take a chance and skip breakfast at the boarding house. He slipped back to his bed, got a couple of cold biscuits and some jerky, ate it, and then went to the stove and had two cups of free, hot coffee. Since the men were going to breakfast in groups, they didn't notice that W. J. didn't go; so he saved a few cents.

As the time drew nearer, the excitement of the sale mounted. The men started gathering around their wagons and breaking open the "hogsheads" so buyers could remove "samples" to examine before they bid on the crop. About eight o'clock the buyers and auctioneer showed up--by then, there was a real :flurry of activity as men jockeyed for- position, yelling obscenities at one another.

W. J. had calculated correctly. The auctioneer came straight to his wagon and removed samples which were passed around. Several of the buyers scowled at the samples but said nothing. The bidding started and was over in seconds. A new buyer had bought W. J.'s crop and paid lots more than he should have for it. He, the inexperienced buyer, in his eagerness to buy, had not paid attention to the quality of the tobacco or to the bids--he outbid himself!

W. J. really felt pleased with himself, but he was also cautious. He decided to collect his money immediately and get out of there before the buyer realized what had happened. So, he took his slip of paper, went. straight to the cashier, and picked up his money--$470.00 in gold and silver coins--and placed it in his near depleted money pouch, which he placed carefully in his overall pocket. By the time he had his money and had said good-by to his friends, his tobacco crop was unloaded. He hitched up his oxen to his wagons, cracked his whip, waved, and was off.

He drove over to Koltinsky's General Store to get a few things which he needed. In addition to the flour, salt, sugar and spices, calico and thread, which his wife had ordered, he bought a new plough share, two-bit ax, and a sack o:f dried fruit. His shopping trip didn't take long, and he was anxious to get started because he wanted to get as close to home as he could that day. It had remained cold, but the sun had come out, and he was afraid it would get warm enough for the roads to thaw. That spelled trouble--even with empty wagons. He loaded his few purchases and moved out--urging the oxen to move faster by cracking the whip over their heads and yelling a few choice words.

He made good time that day and passed the holler where he had camped at about mid afternoon. Even though it was a fine place to camp, he decided to move on. The roads were a little slick but not too bad. He had not even stopped at noon--rather, he had gotten a few handfuls of the dried fruit and eaten it as he walked.

By sundown the fast pace was beginning to tell on the oxen. The lead oxen had started to slow down and tried to leave the road a time or two when they passed cleared fields or farms. W. J. was also getting tired; so, when they came to a patch of trees with a little creek running through them, he pulled the team off the road into the edge of the woods and unhitched them. There were some dried grass and acorns around, and plenty or water; so he decided they wouldn't stray far--particularly, since he didn't feed them.

When the sun went down, it seemed to get 20° colder; and he knew it was going to be a cold night. Since he didn't have a nice cave to sleep in, m decided it would be worth the effort to fix a "warm" bed for the night. Therefore, gathered up a big pile of leaves, limbs, and brush' and lit it. He kept adding to the fire until he had a real bonfire going. He let it burn down, then scraped all the coals away, and cleared about a six-foot square spot on the ground where the fire had been. The earth was hot. He tested every inch for live coals before putting the tarpaulin down on it and, next, the quilts. With the coals which he had scraped away, he made another fire and cooked some sowbelly for supper. By then it was dark. He lay down on his bed and bundled up in the quilts, and the heat from the earth kept him as snug as a bug in a rug! He slept like a baby.

The next morning the wind had come up and it was really cold. It had snowed about 4" during the night. He hurriedly built a small fire and fixed a pot of tea to wash down his hardtack and jerky. He had forgotten and left the piece of sowbelly out the night before, and a wolf or something had come into his camp and stolen it. After a "light" breakfast, he had an urge for a bowel movement (hot tea on dried fruit equals urge); so he scurried off into the woods and made one huge deposit. When he finished, he rolled up his quilts and tarp and put them in the wagon. He beat on the side of the wagon bed and yelled for the oxen. Sure enough" one by one, they emerged from the woods and came trotting up to the wagon.

He fed them a light ration of grain, then hitched them up and It was getting cloudy, and the wind continued to blow. It looked like a winter storm was brewing.

He urged the oxen on; and they probably sensed that they were nearing home for they moved rapidly--for oxen, that is. By late afternoon it had started sleeting, but he was close to his farm and he didn't mind the sleet. He knew that sooner or later it would melt and the land needed the moisture. Soon he rounded a curve and saw his place--the oxen saw it too and speeded up.

One of his boys had seen them approach and spread the word--the whole family came out to meet him, unload the wagons, and unhitch and take care of the oxen. He hugged his wife and they all went inside the house to hear all the news.

W. J. told of all the news he had heard in Hopkinsville and along the way. After he was about run down telling the news, his wife had set the table and they started eating. During the meal he continued to talk between mouth fulls of food and finally got around to bragging on himself for his cunning in maneuvering his wagons to the head of the line so that his scrawny tobacco crop would be the first sold and about how the inexperienced buyer had bid about twice what it was worth. To top off his boasting, he reached into his overall bib pocket to pullout the money pouch and show his family the gold and silver coins which represented the sale price (as well as a year of hard labor).

He found nothing in the pocket--it was empty! He started turning pale as he stood up and searched his other pockets--still nothing~ Next he picked up his coat and searched it--no money! By now he was becoming livid--he yelled at his oldest boy, "Ellis, saddle the black mare for me and put a candle in the saddlebag--I've lost my money and I've got to go find it tonight!"

His wife and daughters tried to calm him down. "W.J.," (or "Pappy"), they said . "It can wait 'til daylight. You're cold and tired--getting out in that sleet and cold might make you sick--we don't need the money that bad."

He was a man possessed, and no amount of urging or coaxing would stop him. He put on his coat and hat and went outside and yelled, "Ellis, hurry up, bring me that horse!" Ellis appeared immediately with the saddled mare; and W. J. mounted, swatted her with his hat, and rode out into the darkness like a demon.

He had the mare on a dead run for the first mile, but she started to slow down, and the sting of the sleet and the cold air began to bring W. J. back to his senses. He let the mare gate down to a walk; and he started thinking finally--Where could I have lost the money? The idea of trying to find it in the darkness became rather futile as he thought it over--the wife and daughters were right. Why shouldn't he get a good night's rest --all cuddled up in the warm feather bed with his wife--maybe get more besides rest--rather than spend a cold, miserable night riding the mare down a dark, dirt road through the woods. He had already convinced himself of the wisdom of waiting until daylight to start his search, also, of taking two or three of his boys along to help, and was about to turn the mare around and head back to the house when his subconscious mind (which had been working on the problem--Where is the money?) flashed the answer to his consciousness. He yelled out in the darkness, "I know where it is" He hit the mare across the flank and put her into a run again.

He was headed for his campsite of the night before. He was sure that the lost money had to be there. He rode the mare hard for a couple of hours, but let her rest enough so that he wouldn't damage her. Finally, he came to what looked like the little patch of woods where he had camped. He pulled the mare in, got off her, got the candle out of the saddlebag, and lit it. After searching around awhile and looking for signs, he finally found the remains of the campfire and his bed.

He then tried to retrace his steps to the place where he had taken the b.m.--but he failed time after time. There were so many trees, and he had gone off into the woods so much more concerned with his urgent problem than with marking the spot that he hadn't paid that much attention.

He again was getting desperate and frantic but finally got control of himself and studied the situation. I guess his subconscious took over again; for he said aloud the second time, "I've got it!" With that he blew out the candle and started sniffing the air like a hound dog on a cold trail--finally, he detected a faint trace of the odor he was searching for and started walking toward it. When it got very strong, he stopped and lit the candle--sure enough, there it was--about four feet in front of him--the most beautiful pile of crap he had seen in his entire life with his money pouch lying in the edge of it!

He said to the mare, "Bess, it's a darn good thing that crap stinks."

CHAPTER 36

CHAWIN' TEBACCER

Most tobacco farmers., in time., became "tobacco worms" themselves. When they stripped the leaves for packing the hogsheads, they got into the habit of setting aside nice-looking, tender leaves and silky-feeling leaves for home consumption. They would then tightly twist them together for some "home twist." Subsequently, this tobacco would be chewed or sometimes crumbled up and smoked in a pipe (usually the corncob variety).

Charlie Cline was such a farmer. He really enjoyed his homemade chawin tobacco and always carried a twist in his britches pocket.

One day he was cultivating a patch of corn in a little field in back of the barn. He had bought a new pair of bib overalls the Saturday before and had been breaking them in that week. There was a rail fence along the north border of the field; and, as he would approach the fence at the end of each trip through the rows of corn, he kept noticing a big lizard on the top rail of the fence. It seemed like the lizard was noticing him too because he would move up the fence a yard or two every time that Charlie completed a row so that he would be directly in line with the row that Charlie was cultivating; and he would cock his head and look right at Charlie as he approached the fence.

Charlie was not afraid of lizards; but he got to noticing that one every time he came up to the fence. After seeing him eight or ten times, he couldn't help thinking about the old lizard all the way to the end of the row and back.

Finally, about-the tenth pass through the corn patch, he came to the end of the row by the rail fence and the lizard was gone. Charlie turned the corner, started down the next row, and felt the lizard crawling up his leg (or, so he thought). He yelled, "Whoa!" to the mule, dropped the plow handles, reached down with his left hand and grabbed the "lizard," reached into his pocket with his right hand and grabbed his pocket knife, which he removed and opened the blade with his teeth. He then held the "lizard" out from his leg, very carefully cut a big swath out of his new overalls which was covering the lizard, threw the cloth and "lizard" to the ground, and "stomped heck out of it." When he picked up the cloth to uncover the stomped lizard, he found instead his twist of tobacco in pipe tobacco form!

Charlie Cline also worked on a railroad section gang for awhile. The other members of the section gang got to noticing Charlie constantly pulling out a big twist of homemade tobacco and taking a big chaw. He seemed to get such a pleasure out of chewing that tobacco and spitting tobacco juice at every grasshopper, spider, or other little critter that came into range.

One by one, the other workmen got to bumming a chaw of tobacco off Charlie. Before long, practically the whole section gang was chewing Charlie's tobacco; and before the day was over, Charlie would be out of tobacco. None of the men offered to pay him anything in return or to buy any store-bought tobacco. They would tell Charlie that his tobacco was so good that every time they tried store-bought tobacco it just didn't match his for flavor and quality! This bragging went on for several weeks until Charlie finally caught on to what was happening.

He lay awake one night trying to figure out how to break that crew of no-goods from consuming all of his tobacco--at the rate they were going, his supply would be gone before winter when he could replenish it. Finally, he hit upon an idea which he figured would work.

The next morning as soon as the section gang got to the area of the roadbed where they were going to work, were laying their lunch boxes on sacks and placing the water barrel under a big oak tree prior to starting work--Charlie pulled out his fresh twist of tobacco and urinated on it right in front of the men. He then took it over to the track and laid it on a rail to dry out. Not a word was spoken.

Charlie had another twist in his pocket, but he didn't dare take a chaw yet. He waited about an hour, then, walked over to the rail and picked up the twist of tobacco. By a sleight-of-hand maneuver, he exchanged it with the uncontaminated twist from which he bit off a big chaw and started chewing. While the men weren't looking, he threw the "doctored" twist in the weeds.

To this day none of the other members of that section gang had asked Charlie for another chaw of tobacco or chewed any more tobacco--Period! One of them that day finally got the courage to ask, "Charlie, why did you do that?" To which Charlie replied, "That's the way you cure chawin I tobacco--I thought everybody knew that."

CHAPTER 37

UNCLE BOB'S FLYING MACHINE

The country folk and hill folk in Kentucky weren't much different from folk the world over from the beginning of time. They had their likes and dislikes-- their goals, their dreams, their ambitions.

This story is about one of the really big dreamers with a major ambition--back in time in the Thomas family tree. He was called Uncle Bob Thomas, and his ambition was to fly like a buzzard.

Uncle Bob didn't have any formal education, but they say he was real smart. He used to sit for hours and watch the buzzards circling around overhead and wish that he could join them. They seemed so graceful and free--floating across the sky.

He would go back to the cabin, take a turkey quill with elderberry ink, and draw picture after picture of his flying machine. The version which he always came back to, after trying different ideas, was to make some big wings to strap on his arms--the feathers which he would get from the buzzards, of course. He knew where there was an old buzzard roost, and there were hundreds of feathers on the ground under the roost trees.

Uncle Bob didn't keep his dream and ambition to himself either. He used to take his drawings to Eddyville, when he would go to town, and show them to anybody who would look and listen. All the folks that knew him kind of passed it off and felt sorry for the old man who was teched in the head some. The very idea--thinking he could fly.

There was one supporter, however, who kept the faith. That was Si Brown, his neighbor and friend of many years. Si kept encouraging him to build his flying machine. And it was Si's urging that finally got Uncle Bob started to building his flying machine. Like most of the early inventors in the flying era before Orville and Wilbur finally showed us how it should be done, Uncle Bob figured that the way to fly was to transform a man into a bird--as near as possible--and, therein was the key that would unlock his attachment to the ground and let him soar across the sky--like a buzzard.

Uncle Bob had Si as his able assistant when he actually began construction on his flying contraption--which, by now, was well-defined in his mind's eye and was modeled, of course, from a buzzard. He and So gathered wire, twine, pitch, and the buzzard feathers together and built the wings which Bob intended to strap to his arms and fly.

After several days they finally had the project completed--but, Uncle Bob spent another day fiddling around with it, trimming a feather here, adding one there, etc. Actually, he was stalling for time. The next day was Sunday, and Uncle Bob could see two advantages to waiting until then to fly--first, it would be a holy day; and, in the back of Uncle Bob's mind, he figured he might need some help from upstairs. Second, he could announce the "flight" at church and have a big crowd to watch him take off. (He would show those who had doubted him and made fun of him.)

At church on Sunday morning Uncle Bob got up and "testified"; and, in his testimony to the Lord, he managed to work in his announcement that at two o'clock sharp he was going to fly off the top of Copeland Bluff and sail up to the clouds like a buzzard!

As expected, by one-thirty o'clock everyone and his dog for miles around was gathered at Copeland Bluff to watch the miracle of flight (or disaster of landing). Almost all collected on the top of the bluff because the road ran across its top, and the foot of the bluff rested in Piney Creek. A few of the younguns had climbed down on the ledges to get a better view of Uncle Bob as he sailed over.

At about a quarter till two, Uncle Bob and Si drove up in the buggy to mixed hoots and cheers. Uncle Bob got down, strutted around a minute or two, and made a short speech about the miracle that was about to take place. Meanwhile, Si was very carefully taking the flying contraption out of the buggy and getting it laid out so he could "rig up" Uncle Bob when he was through strutting and crowing.

Uncle Bob came strutting back like a banty rooster and said, "Si, the time has come for me to fly--strap on my wings." Si very gently lifted the wings and strapped them to Uncle Bob's arms and then strapped the guiders to his legs.

When Uncle Bob stepped from behind the buggy in his buzzard wings, "again, a roar of' laughter, horselaughs, cheers, jeers, etc., rose up from the crowd. By now, Uncle Bob was psyched up sufficiently so that he didn't pay them any mind. He waddled straight to the edge of the bluff' like a man of destiny--with faithful Si right in his footsteps. He paused at the edge of the bluff for a moment--and then leaped out into history.

As he was tumbling through space toward the obvious landing in Piney Creek, Si was shouting at the top of his voice, "Flap, Bob, flap like a buzzard!" Kersplash!

CHAPTER 38

SPOOKS AND GOBLINS

Mankind has always had to cope with fear and much has been written on the subject. Generally, man fears the unknown--things he can't comprehend. Even the good book makes mention of fear in several places--nevertheless, fear remains and will be with us forever.

They say that one of the principal movers of men before the wheel was invented was fear. A man would be walking through the woods; a bear or something would jump out; and the man would transport himself by foot a considerable distance in a very short period of time!

In the backwoods, pranksters used fear- as the basis of many a prank. Some of those pranks and tales which bring on "fear" have been told often by my Dad-- a few which I remember are as follows:

The Newsome Hollow Ghost

The road from Macedonia to Cross Roads went along the edge of Newsome Hollow. The hollow was very deep, wide, and heavily wooded--as was the area on both sides of the road. There were many tales of travelers at night who met their fate at the hands of haints, spooks, goblins, or other creatures that came up out of the hollow on dark nights to prey on unsuspecting travelers. Whether you believed the stories or not--it was still frightening to travel that road alone at night--and still is if you are afoot.

The Josey's place was about four miles north of Newsome Hollow, and they were the nearest farm to the hollow. They say the Josey boys were full of mischief and weren't afraid of the devil himself. One of their favorite tricks was to rig up a "ghost" by Newsome Hollow and scare the bejabbers out of folks that passed that way after dark.

My Dad chuckles as he reminisces about spending one Saturday night with the Josey boys and helping them with their favorite prank which was accomplished as follows;

After dark they would tie a rope between two trees--about fifteen feet above ground level. They would place a pulley on the rope and attach a sheet (dangling) from the pulley. At the top of the sheet, they would tie a piece of string and run it off into the woods. The boys would take a saw with them and hide up in the woods when they heard an unsuspecting traveler approach--and you could usually hear one coming for quite a distance; for, if he were alone he would always be singing or whistling; if there were two or more, they would be talking loudly.

On this particular night the first customers were a man and woman in a buggy. The boys didn1t know exactly who they were but thought they sounded like Mr. and Mrs. Barnes from Piney Grove. It really didn't matter--the boys waited until the horse which was pulling the buggy was nearly under the rope and then the following happened:

First, Sam Josey started jiggling the string enough to make the sheet dance a little and start moving slowly across the road on the rope.

Second, Cliff Josey started "playing" the saw so that it made a moaning and wailing noise.

Third, my Dad started making moaning and groaning noises--with a high-pitched wail thrown in for good measure.

And, somewhere during this cycle in the woods, the following cycle was simultaneously taking place on the road:

Old mare, "Neighhh!" (and reared up)

Wife, "Eeeeeck l A ghost."

Husband, "Whoa, Belle~ Darn~ Giddyup!" (cracked with the whip)

Then, thundering hoofbeats fading into the distance followed by hilarious laughter by the three boys up in the woods.

Dad says this same thing happened two or three additional times during that night, but the merriment was short-lived because of this incident:

About ten o'clock they heard a lone rider coming down the road. He was singing "She was only a bootlegger's daughter--But I love her still," at the top of his drunken lungs. When the boys heard him coming, they figured that this "scare" was going to be the "highlight" of the night; and, as it turned out--it was

But, not exactly as they had planned. When they started jiggling the sheet and moaning, the rider stopped his horse and yelled, "Monk, is that you?" Then silence, except for the saw's moaning. The rider "hicked" and said in even a more drunken voice, "Monk, I've warned you about pranking with me when I've been drinking." (Evidently, he had been a previous victim at the hands of someone named Monk.)

More silence which was shattered by BANG! BANG! BANG! Bullets came crashing through the treesl Another momentary silence followed by the noise of three scared boys fleeing through the woods and the loud, drunken laughter of a rider who had turned the tables on them.

Hoot Owls

Hoot owls and screech owls can scare the bejabbers out of you also when you are alone in the country at night, and they let out a hoot or screech in the immediate vicinity. Dad tells of the reaction of one of his younger brothers that was faced with this situation when he was about nine or ten years old.

The old milk cow had gotten out of the pasture and wandered off into the woods. Three of the boys were sent to fetch her about dark. They decided that they would have a better chance of finding her if they split up. Calvin, the youngest went to the southeast, my dad was to go south, and his other brother, Stallard, was to go southwest. 'They agreed to either meet back of the woods at the bridge over Montgomery Creek or to yell real loud if they spotted the cow.

Dad and Stallard, being older, walked faster and got to the bridge about the same time. Neither had seen the cow. They waited and waited, but Calvin didn't show up. They started to call him, but the woods remained silent. Finally, they decided that they had better forget the cow and start looking for Calvin. They started a wide circle out to the northeast in hopes they would come across him--which they

did. They had traveled about a mile, stopping ever now and then to listen, and finally heard him crying off in the woods. Both of the older boys were relieved--and, now their true nature set in. They decided that they would slip up on Calvin and give him a real scare. About the time they had slipped up close enough to let out a growl and shake the brush to scare Calvin, a big, old hoot owl cut loose in a big tree overhead, "Who! Who! Who are you?"

Calvin stopped his crying; and the woods were deathly silent--then, the owl hooted again, "Who! Who! Who are you?"

Calvin said in a barely audible voice, "I'm Lib Thomas' boy, Calvin--out looking for a lost cow."

The older brothers couldn't help laughing real loud, and a happy family reunion was held on the spot. Calvin grew up with that story told on him dozens of times--he still blushes when it's told.

The White-faced Calf

As the boys got older, one of the "necessary" properties that each had to own was a pistol. This was a sign that a boy had become a man. (Today the symbol is the car.) These pistols were really the antitoxin to the "fear" which I've been talking about. Traveling alone on those dark country roads could be scary--and carrying a pistol (thy rod and they staff) relieved part of the tension.

Contrary to popular belief, the pistols weren't used often except maybe to shoot a snake or shoot at a squirrel or something, and most of the men weren't too good a, shot--with the pistols, that is. (Ammunition was too precious to waste practicing.) (However, most men were excellent marksmen with the rifle.)

One night my Uncle Harley (Dad's oldest brother) was returning to the farm after a courting trip to the Orange's place. That night, they had sat and talked about ghosts and goblins; and he had that on his mind as he rode up to the barn and unsaddled his horse.

When he had taken care of his horse and turned it out in the pasture, he started around the barn toward the house. As he turned the corner, rounding the barn, he saw a ghost standing next to the barn and looking straight at him. Instinctively, he pulled out his pistol and emptied it and ran yelling to the house.

The shots and his yelling woke everyone up; and, by the time he got to the house, Granddad was standing in the door in his nightshirt with a kerosene lamp in one hand and his double-barreled shotgun in the other.   Uncle Harley nearly bowled him over as he crowded through the door.

Granddad said, "Harley, what's the matter? You look like a haint is after you!" Harley said, "I seen a ghost--down by the barn." Granddad laughed and said, "I thought I raised you better than that--you're practically a grown man and still afraid of a ghost--I'll declare! Come with me and let's go see that ghost." Harley resisted; but after Granddad threatened to whack him one, he reluctantly agreed to come along.

They walked down to the barn with Granddad in the lead carrying the light (kerosene lamp). When they went around the side of the barn, there lay the "ghost" stone dead--it was a prize white-faced bull calf that Granddad had aimed to raise for a bull.

Needless to say, they enjoyed veal for a few days; and Uncle Harley never lived that story down either.

CHAPTER 39

UNCLE DEWEY'S MOTORSICKLE

My Uncle Dewey never cared much about farming and he was scared to death of the coal mines so when he got out of high school he packed up his clothes in a carpet bag and hitched a ride on a freight trail. He ended up in the big city of Chicago, Illinois and got a job at a meat packing plant. He worked hard and saved his money but he could never meet any girls or get a date. His problem was that he as so bashful. If he got around girls and got to looking at them his imagination would take over and his thing would start swelling. He would blush, stick his hand in his pocket and hold it against his leg and get away from the females as quick as he could - blushing as he left.

One day he was wandering around his neighborhood and saw a bunch of girls gathered around a man wearing a black leather jacket. He joined the crowd and when he got close enough he saw that the man was a straddle of a two wheeled machine that resembled a big wheeled bicycle. The man was taking off bits of paper from a sheet, writing numbers on them, and handing them to the girls.

He recognized one of the girls in the crowd as one who worked at the packing plant with him. Her name was Suzy Black, and Dewey worked his way through the crowd and finally was able to get close to her. He tapped her on the shoulder and said "Hi Suzy - would you please tell me what is going on here?" Suzy replied "Well hello Dewey - What are you doing here? Dewey said "I was just wandering around the neighborhood and spotted this crowd and came over to see what was going on - but can't figure it out". Suzy got him by the hand and led him away from the clamoring crowd to a park bench and they sat down. Suzy said "That's George Zappus from the packing plant. He bought that Harley Davidson motorcycle and he is going to give all the girls a ride - one at a time, he gave each a number and will take them for a ride in the order of the numbers.

About that time there was a loud roar as George started the motorcycle and rode off with a girl riding behind him - her arms wrapped around him and holding on tight. Suzy said "See how that girl is holding tight - she is thrilled with that ride - all girls just love to ride on a motorcycle - it vibrates and really gets them all sexed up". Dewey asked "Really?" Suzy said "Really!"

Dewey started asking questions about motorcycles -

*Where do you buy them?

*How much do they cost?

*Who can teach you how to ride one?, etc., etc.

Suzy said, "There is a Harley Davidson dealer about 3 blocks from here - on Wisconsin Avenue. Most people think they are the best made. I've heard they will teach you how to ride if you buy one from them." Dewey said "Thanks Suzy - I'm going straight over there". Suzy said "If you get one, let me be your first passenger." Dewey said "It's a deal."

Dewey walked to the dealership and peeked in to the showroom. It was full of shiny new motorcycles - all sizes and colors. He went inside and the owner himself, Zeke Czeyski, met him and introduced himself and asked if he could help him. Dewey told him he was thinking about buying a motorcycle but he didn't know if he could afford one and that he didn't know how to ride - "How much do they cost?" Zeke said they ranged from about $400 up to $8,000. He asked Dewey "How much can you afford? Dewey said - "Maybe $500 - but I want a big one. Zeke asked "Would you consider a used one?" Dewey said "Sure, if it is in good shape".

Zeke said "Tell you what I'll do - "The highway patrol has ordered 20 new bikes and they are due here next week. I'll personally inspect their trade-ins and pick you out a good one - service it, remove their decals, etc and shine it up - and let you have it for $500 cash." Dewey said "And teach me how to ride?" Zeke said "I'll have one of my employees teach you." Dewey said "I'll think on it and come back next Saturday."

All he could think about the following week was whether or not to spend his hard earned savings on a motorcycle. He asked his follow workers for their advice. Charlie, who worked next to him was the clincher. He told Dewey, if he bought a motorcycle and learned how to ride, he would get more smack madam than he could shake a stick at. (Dewey thought - that's what Suzy was trying to tell me).

The following Saturday, Dewey was at the Harley Davidson dealership when they opened the door - $500 cash in pocket. Zeke took him to the shop and showed him a large white Harley that he picked out for him. He cranked it up and it sounded wonderful (they had put a straight exhaust on it - it was very loud) Dewey bought it and they completed the paperwork and Dewey paid for it.

Next came the riding lessons - conducted by a mechanic named Ned. Ned asked "Can you ride a bicycle?" "Dewey said "No." Can you drive a car? "No." What can you ride? "I can ride a mule." Fine, hop on and I'll ride behind you - you steer and learn to balance and turn. When you can do that everything else is simple.

By mid afternoon Ned said - "It's time for a solo ride." Much to Dewey's amazement, he was about to start his new Harley and ride around the block by himself - although he never got beyond 2nd gear. Ned said "You got a license?" Dewey said "Why no - do I need one?" Ned said "No you need two" You are going to have to leave the motorcycle here and come back any day next week and I'll go with you to get your licenses. "How much?" Inquired Dewey, Ned said "Forty" - then rethought and said "Bring fifty, just in case." Dewey said "Is Wednesday afternoon ok?" (He would get paid Wednesday). Ned said "Fine - see you Wed P.M." Let me give you a pamphlet that I want you to memorize before Wed. Dewey could hardly stand the suspense the next few days. All he could think about was his new motor sickle (that is what country folk called them) - and the pleasure he believed it would deliver.

Wednesday finally came and when he got paid he asked his boss for the afternoon off. His boss gave permission and he headed for the dealership. Ned drove him to the license place and took him inside. He bought the metal plates for the motorcycle and took the written test - which he easily passed. They went outside and the police officer instructed him what he expected him to do - start, ride through a marked course, do a couple of stops, etc. While he was riding he saw Ned slip the officer a $5 bill. He passed, took Ned back to the dealership, filled the gas tank, and rode southwest toward Kankakee. When he got outside the built up area he turned on to a rural road and got braver and braver. He was learning how to handle that motorcycle.

When the sun started to go down he headed back toward Chicago. As he got into the city he realized that he did not know how to get to the boarding house where he lived. He also realized he had no place to keep his new motorcycle. He stopped at the first Gulf station and bought some maps and at the first hardware store and bought a strong chain - about 6 feet and a master lock. He studied the city maps and figured a route home and when he got there he chained his new prize to a large tree in the front yard.

The next day at work he was describing the thrill of his ride in the country side to Suzy and she asked "Will you take me for a ride tonight? He said "Yes - we can stop somewhere and eat supper too."

After work Dewey and Suzy walked the 12 blocks from the plant to the boarding house. when Suzy saw the white and black Harley she went plumb wild. "It's beautiful" she told Dewey. Dewey took his lunch pail to his room and returned with the key and unlocked the motorcycle. He straddled it and kick started it. They rode West Southwest out of Chicago and once they cleared the built up area they rode down the farm roads through corn fields mostly. Suzy really snuggled up to him and he could feel her ample breasts pressing into his back. The next thing he felt was her hand on his thing. They came to a wooded area along a stream and she spoke into his ear - "Dewey darling - let's stop here." He pulled off into the woods and before he came to a stop she had unzipped his pants and was fondling his thing - which by now was so hard a cat couldn't scratch it.

Dewey switched off the Harley, lowered the kick stand, swung off and he and Suzy took a romp in the hay (actually - a romp in the leaves). Dewey lay there panting and grinning. That was the best feeling he had ever had. Suzy said "Wasn't that good?" Dewey answered "It was better than good - it was terrific." It was getting dark so they got back on the Harley and headed for home.

During the next few weeks Dewey took Suzy for several rides out in the countryside and on each trip they would locate a secluded spot to romp in the hay. On a few Saturdays, Dewey joined the Zappus' crowd in Chicago and gave some other girls a ride and a couple of them a romp as well.

One day in late summer the boss came by at work and said "Dewey, the plant is going to be shut down for a week for some maintenance work - starting Monday. The company will add a hundred dollar bonus to your check this week to tide you over until you come back to work a week from Monday." Dewey said "Fine, I think I'll take a trip back home to Kentucky next week then. I need to go see my folks".

On Saturday morning Dewey packed up a few clothes and put them in the saddle bags and headed south. The trip was uneventful and just before dark he drove up to his folks farm near Piney Grove. They were happy to see him and were mighty impressed with his <u>motor</u> <u>sickle</u> - that's what country folks called a motorcycle (as I told you previously).

Word of Dewey's arrival and the shiny Harley Davidson spread rapidly and after church most of the girls in the area found some reason to go to the Chambers farm. They all gathered around the shiny Harley Davidson and hinted they wanted to go for a ride. Dewey got a pencil and piece of paper and started tearing off pieces and giving each girl a number - just as he had observed Mr. Zappus doing it in Chicago.

A few of the local boys had also come by and when they figured out what Dewey was up to they became very jealous - and angry. Rufus Burns said, "Boys, I got an idea on how we can stop that City Slicker before he steals our women." They said "What is your idea?" Rufus said - "Let me borrow whatever money you got on you and I'll show you." A hat was passed and Rufus counted the take - two dollars and sixty seven cents($2.67).

He broke through the crowd of young women and confronted Dewey with "Dewey, I'll be you can't ride that motor sickle of yours up Baldface Mountain inside of ten minutes." Dewey had hunted on Baldface Mountain (which was really a tall hill with exposed sandstone on its top) and knew he could climb it to the top on his powerful Harley Davidson in no more than five minutes so he said "Rufus, I hate to take your money but if you insist - I'll bet with you. How much? Rufus said "Two dollars and sixty seven cents." Dewey laughed and said "Make it five dollars and you got a bet." Rufus couldn't be embarrassed in front of all the girls so he said "O.K. - five bucks." (He had no idea where he would get the other $2.33 if he lost - but he was purty sure he wouldn't lose.)

Baldface Mountain was about a mile down the road so everyone went down to the base of the mountain. Cindy Mitchell, the preachers daughter was elected "judge" and the rules were very simple. If Dewey rode up the mountain and appeared on the bald spot on top with his motor sickle within ten minutes from his start - he won.

Everyone was very excited as Dewey straddled the Harley, kick started it, and raced the motor a few times - it was very loud. Cindy had Joe Lubell's pocket watch and when it came up to 1:30 she shouted "Go!"

The engine roared even louder as Dewey started through the trees and up the side of the mountain. In seconds the brush got thicker and thicker but he powerful Harley plowed through it. There was no road that he could find.

Meanwhile, further up that side of the mountain Zeke Smith (who lived on the side of the mountain) was just finishing eating and his wife, Lizzy, asked "Pa - what in tarnation is all the racket down below us?" Zeke said "Don't know but I'll get my double barrel shotgun and go set on the porch. If it's a bear or something I'll shoot it with both barrels if it gets close to the house. (The front porch was high on stilts and Zeke had a good view of the side of the mountain.)

The noise got louder and louder and the bushes were shaking mighty - just below the cabin KBOOM! KBOOM! went the shot gun.

Ma yelled "Did you get it pa? What was it?

Pa yelled back at her "Don't rightly know - but whatever it was, it dang sure turned loose of that young feller it had a hold of".

F. SEXY STORIES

I'm afraid I've mislead you with the description of the following stories. By today's standards they ain't sexy at all. You would probably find more sex today in a kid's book.

What you got to keep in mind was in the old days anything about sex was verboten. The puritanical influence still dominated. My mamma drilled it into my brain that if I done it before I was married; my peedi wink (that's what she called my thing) would fall off.

On second thought, there may have been a few sexy stories whispered among the adults - I just didn't get to hear them. (I do remember one time at a family reunion - my Aunt Less walked up to my dad and asked "Tom, do you know what a bird can do that a man can't?" Dad said "No, less - What?" - "Whistle thru his pecker" answered Aunt Less and everyone within earshot burst into laughter as dad turned red as a beet.

Anyway, here are a few borderline sexy tales:

<u>Chapter</u>

40   A Sure Bet

41   Fast Women

42   Thou Shalt Not

43   That's One

44   Fooled Her

45   Pinch and Judy

46   Beautiful Dreamer

CHAPTER 40

A SURE BET

There were several stories about newlyweds--most of which dealt with sex. Since I determined before starting this book that subject would be avoided as much as possible. I've been forced to omit a few humorous tales.

This particular story has to do with determining the "head of the household" during the period right after the honeymoon.

Seth Hawkins and his new bride, Bess, had finished supper and were sitting around the table sipping coffee. Bess said, "Seth, honey, why don't you wash dishes for me?"

Seth was almost caught off guard by the honeyed question; but he wasn't quite--he said, "Heck, honey, that's woman work--I'm a <u>man</u>." Bess said, "You sure are--but that ain't going to do you no good tonight if you don't wash the dirty dishes."

Seth could see that he was trapped and .it was going to be hard to win that argument. He tried to "sweet talk" his way out of his predicament--but without much success. He did mellow Bess enough that she finally said, "Well, sweetheart, It'll tell you what we can do to settle this agreement." He asked, "What?" Bess said, "Have a contest."

Seth thought for a minute and concluded that he could beat that frail, little thing in any contest; so he said, "That's fine with me--what kind of contest?"

Bess explained that they would go out by the side of the house and urinate on the wall--the one who could make a wet spot the highest on the wall being the winner; and the loser, of course, would have to wash the dishes.

Seth smiled and thought that his frail, little bride had given in because she obviously didn't have a chance in such a contest. He got up, kissed her on the cheek, and said, "O. K., honey, let's go have that contest so we can get the dishes washed and get to bed." She smiled back and said, "O.K., sugar, let's go."

They lived out in the country so there wasn't much danger of anybody seeing them. Bess pulled down her pants, pulled up her skirt, and cut loose. She made a wet place on the wall about 3 feet from the ground.

By now, Seth's smile was taking on the appearance of a smirk as he pulled his instrument out and aimed it at an angle to hit well above Bess's mark. . Bess yelled, "Wait, Seth! I forgot to tell you the rules-
No hands allowed."

They say that Seth was the first man in West Kentucky with dishwasher's hands.

CHAPTER 41

FAST WOMEN

Clay Page was one of the best tobacco growers in Caldwell County. As well he should have been – all he did was work his tobacco patch. He was an old bachelor, and the rumor was that he was one of the very few 40 year old male virgins in the state – if not the universe.

Any time he tried to join the boys gathered around the pot bellied stove telling tall tales – they would kid him so much about women, etc. that he would turn tail and run. Clay always had money and a fairly new pickup truck and he soon learned that he could throw a wash tub in the truck, drive to Mannington and purchase a case of "legal" beer, ice it down in the wash tub and then drive to Orange's store – he could become "One of the Boys".

It was nearing Christmas and Clay had taken his tobacco to the auction at Hoptown, the price of tobacco was up that year and his crop brought near 7 thousand dollars. He took the check by Planters Bank and deposited sixty five hundred and got four hundred and something in cold cash. He rolled the money up with a fifty on the outside and put it in his pocket.

The Christian County Fair and Tobacco Jubilee was going full swing and Clay decided that since it was still early in the day, he would visit the fair before driving back to the farm. He wandered all over the fair grounds and was attracted to the traveling carnival that had set up in the Northeast corner of the fair grounds. He wandered over that way and spotted the old "baseball throw" booth. (The one where you throw a baseball at three leaded milk bottles and try to knock them down.) If you do, you win a stuffed giraffe or something. Old Clay had a good arm and had won two or three stuffed animals but spent all his change.

He reached for his roll of big money at the same time that two people walked up – from different directions. Beatrice Smith came slinking up from one way and Ralph Trueheart (one of the Orange Store regulars) came up from another.

Beatrice was one of the girls from Miss Phoebe's cat house just south of Hoptown. She was one of the better looking and best known hookers in that end of the state – but Clay didn't know who she was:

Clay and Ralph exchanged "Howdies" and Clay pulled out his big roll of money and paid for four more games. Beatrice's eyes got real big when she saw that roll of bills – particularly the fifty on top. She immediately struck up a conversation with Clay and started bragging on him when he showed her the stuffed animals. He gave them to her and she grabbed him and gave him first a kiss on the lips – he put his arms around her and she next gave him another kiss – except this time it was a French kiss. In the meantime, she was rubbing it all over him and he started to sweat. He finally got loose and tried to throw some more baseballs but couldn't hit the back of the tent – much less the milk bottles.

He finally gave up and Beatrice said "I'm hungry." Clay said, "Why don't we all (including Ralph in his offer) go down to Bubba's Barbeque and eat. They accepted and everyone went to their vehicle and met at Bubba's.

When they sat down in a booth at Bubba's, Ralph and Clay sat opposite each other and Beatrice scooted in next to Clay – showing a lot of skin in so doing. She got real close to ole Clay and continued sweet talking him as she placed her hand on his leg – just above the knee – and rubbed him all the way up to his thing. She rubbed it to.

They finished eating and were sipping beer and smoking cigarettes when some slick headed dude in a seersucker suit came in the door and motioned for Beatrice. She told Clay and Ralph "Bye" and left. They sat and talked awhile and Ralph said he was going by Orange's Store on the way home. Clay said he would go through Mannington, get some beer, and join him at Orange's. They both left.

When Clay drove up to Orange's Store, Ralph along with the usual whittle and spit crew were there – gathered around the stove.

Ralph and his beer joined them. Several of them encouraged Clay to tell them about that fast female he had met at the fair. (Ralph had already told them part of the story).

Clay, grateful for the opportunity to discuss sex and females with the big boys, told of his experience in great detail – stretching a point here and there when he thought it would improve his image.

At the conclusion, he proudly stated "You know, boys, I'm sure I could have got me some of that – don't you Ralph?"

Ralph said "Heck yes – all you would have had to done was to peel that fifty of your bankroll and give it to her."

CHAPTER 42

THOU SHALT NOT......

Most of the country folk were of high morals, God-fearing, and straight laced-
-particularly, when measured by today's standards. I didn't say there was no evil
and sin--there was. However, there were unique ways to cope with it--
particularly certain sins. This story deals with one of the most dastardly deeds
imaginable in those days--adultery.

Sam Bond was a dark-headed, handsome cuss that had a way with the women.
You know the type--he would look at a gal; and she would just melt. Sam had
two problems associated with his natural ability. First, he was a braggart.
Second, he failed to use discretion. Sam got a lesson at the Dawson Daylight
Mine Camp which broke him from both problems. I've heard Dad tell this tale
many times.

Sam had been working at the mines for a couple of months and living at the
bachelors' quarters in the mine camp. He didn't have any close friends in camp,
and that didn't seem to bother him. He was never there anyway to take part in the
bull sessions or domino and card games--he was always out chasing skirts! Once
in awhile, just before payday, he might hang around for a day or two, but usually
spent his spare time cleaning and polishing his Model A roadster.

Whenever he was around the other bachelors the few times he was around the bachelor quarters, he took delight in bragging on his exploits with the girls. Naturally, the other bachelors were jealous and hated his guts--particularly, when one of the females he might mention happened to be one that they knew and respected--or coveted--or had tried and failed themselves --or whatever.

Sam finally went too far, and the others decided it was time for action. One Sunday afternoon Sam was getting all slicked up to go courting as usual and was in a particularly bragging mood. It seems that he had been making with a married woman who lived in St. Charles and whose husband travelin salesman. He had hinted to the other bachelors that he was going a courtin the married gal that night--right after her husband left the house for the road. They kept quizzing him--trying to find out her identity; but I just laughed and kept bragging and ignoring their questions.

Finally, he was about ready to leave; and he decided to really shake them up. He announced, "Boys, I'll tell you what I'm going to do--I'm going to give you one more clue; and, if any of you is a real stud Hoss, you might figure out the answer. If you will go out to my Model A roadster and take off the left front hubcap, you'll have your answer--if you're man enough to figure it out." Sam was in his glory as he reared back and laughed at them as they all scrambled out to his car.

He walked out to the car just as Bub Ford was removing the hubcap--which fell to the ground trailed by a pair of--ladies' panties. All the men looked at one another in disbelief and then at Sam. Sam grinned, leaned over and picked up the hubcap and replaced it, then opened the door, got into his Model A roadster, and drove off with the rest of the bachelors standing in a circle around the panties.

Finally, Frank Towne said, "Can anybody tell who them things belong to? Everyone was silent. Frank picked them up and held them out in front of him for all to see--then said, "Anybody got any ideas?" More silence! The silence was broken in a few moments by little Buddy Hatem, who said, "Judging from the size of them things, I'd say she ain't too big." Hank Roll laughed and said, "Heck, Buddy--ain' t you ever seen a woman dress before--them things stretch.1! (After a heated exchange between Buddy and Hank, it came out that Buddy, in fact, had never seen a woman dress or undress; and the only time that Hank had witnessed such an event was once at the gymnasium in Nebo when he was there at a girls basketball game and peeped through a hole in the wall between the dressing room. Anyway, everyone finally decided that they had better go back inside the bachelors' quarters and take the object with them before somebody drove by and saw them with it.

Once safely inside, they passed the object around among themselves for close personal inspection--but no answers were forthcoming. When they got to Buddy, he examined them very carefully and said, "I still say she ain't very big and she sure must smell nice too--did anybody notice the smell?" More laughter and poking fun at Buddy .

Everybody sat around for an hour or so trying to solve the mystery. Several likely candidates were proposed; but nobody could say for certain who the rightful owner of them cute, little, pink panties was -but., they figured that Buddy might have a good point about the size and that narrowed the candidates down somewhat.

Things went along as normal for several days, and nothing much was said about the mystery which Sam had dropped on them Sunday. Everyone continued to study about it though--you could tell by the way they kept coming by Bud's room to casually chat--all the time sneaking glances at the evidence which Bud had been assigned to guard.

The following Saturday afternoon Bud came running into the bachelors' quarters yelling, "I saw her! I saw her! I know who she is!" Everyone crowded around to hear the news. When things settled down" he announced, "That Sam has been slipping around with Bob Smith's wife, Bubbles." Someone asked ""How do you know?" Bud replied "I was in the Rexall Drug Store in Madisonville this morning; and she was there--buying some perfume. I got a whiff of it" and it smelled just like them things. Also, she was telling the clerk at the store that Bud was never home since he had taken the traveling salesman's job right after Easter.

Everyone got to thinking about it" and finally Zeb- Walsh said" "That shore makes sense to me--I've knowed Bubbles for a long time--used to court her some before she met and married Bob--and I'd say she was that type of a hussy."

They sat around for awhile longer; and" finally" John French spoke up, "I've been figuring how we can get even with ole Sam."· "How?" came the question of .the boys. He continued, "Bob is a big, gruff feller; and I expect that somebody has already told Sam how tough he is. Why don't we call Sam, say we are Bob, and scare hell out of him?" Everyone agreed that this would be a real pleasure. They selected Claude Sisk to do the talking since Sam didn't know him, and, since Claude had a deep and rough voice. The trap was there was a telephone on the wall in the hallway of the bachelors' quarters (which were more or less a dormitory), and they decided that Claude would go use the phone at the company store to call Sam on the bachelors' quarters phone. When Sam got in that night, the signal was passed to Claude; and the telephone started jangling. Sam even answered the phone. (He usually did, for he got the most calls.)

Claude related the conversation as follows:

Claude, "Sam?"

Sam, "Yep, who's this?"

Claude, "I'm Bubbles' husband, and she's just got through telling me everything. I'm so mad I could kill you and her too--but, I'm smart enough to know that I'd get sent to the pen in Eddyville if I did that. So--I've just finished beating heck out of her and you're next if you are a man, you'll meet me out in the yard in front of your place in about ten minutes and we get it on" CLICK!

The rest of the boys were crowded up in Bud's room 'peeping out the cracked door at Sam while the conversation was going on. They say that Sam kept getting paler and paler and finally looked white as a sheet as he hung up the receiver and almost ran to his room, slammed the door shut, and locked it.

In about eight or ten minutes, Claude came in; and everyone was giggling and grinning almost beyond control with Bud shushing them so they wouldn't spoil the remainder of the well-planned plan to break Sam from chasing around with married women and bragging so.

One of the boys had brought a dynamite cap from the mine and had it ready. Claude and he slipped down the hallway to Sam's door. Claude banged on the door and yelled in his meanest voice, "Sam Bond, you low-down, cowardly son of a cur dog--come out and fight like the man you say you are! Come on out, or I'm coming in! Just what I thought--you're yeller through and through! (with that--Claude banged and kicked on the door some more.) Pause! Then Claude said , "0. K., I'll shoot the darn lock off then."

The other boy was ready--BANG~---went the blasting cap! ---Slight pause. CRASH., Tinkle! --came noises from Sam' s room.

During this melodrama all of the other boys had slipped out of Bud's room and down to Ken Jones' room, which was next to Sam's. When they heard all of the racket in Sam's room, they ran to Ken's window in time to see Sam pick himself up from the lawn under his window and take off like a deer. They said he cleared the five-foot hedge by a good foot.

Everyone laughed and laughed so hard that tears came to some eyes. That was absolutely the funniest thing that any had ever seen or heard of. They had flat taught Sam a lesson that he would not soon forget!

Ole Sam disappeared; although his Model A roadster sat out front. After about a week the boys began to get worried about him. They were afraid they had scared him to death! All of them inquired around for him; but nobody had seen him; and he hadn't been to work either. The following Sunday afternoon they had decided that someone was going to have to go see his folks in Clifty and tell them or his disappearance--when the backdoor screen door squeaked; in slipped Sam!

Everyone breathed a sigh of relief to see him but sucked in a shocked breath at the same time at his looks! He was bandaged up so much he looked like a mummy. (His dive through the window had been disastrous!)

They all crowded around him; and Bud asked the question first, "Sam, what; in heck happened to you?" Sam said, "Bud, I was in this terrible car wreck a week ago;. and it nearly killed me--I've been in the hospital in Madisonville!" Bud said, "Whose car--yours has been parked out front?" Bud said, "I was out Saturday night a week ago with this feller from Providence that you all don't know; and we went off Dead Man's Curve and turned over. I tell you--it was terrible!"

Everyone had kept a straight face up to now; but the more Sam talked, the harder the task became; so the crowd started breaking up and disappearing by twos and threes into rooms where they "broke up" the minute they closed the door. Finding Sam not too bad for wear- and relieved at the news--the whole incident became even funnier. And it even got funnier the next several days.

According to Bud; early the next morning Sam came to his room and asked him to tell the boss about the accident--also, to bring him some bologna, bread, mustard, and sweet milk that night. Bud did, of course, and repeated the delivery a day or two later. Sam stayed locked up in his room for about a week--living on baloney sandwiches.

The next week he took off some of the bandages and went back to work. However, he always waited for several of the boys to join them on the trip to the mine. Each night, he would wait around the mine tunnel for several of the boys who lived in the bachelors' quarters and would sneak into the middle of them to walk back to the bachelors' quarters. He always went straight to his room and locked his door--wouldn't even answer the phone!

On payday--Sam disappeared again. This time for good! He took his belongings and Model A coupe. He wasn't heard from for many years.

I don't know whether it is true or not, but word finally got back to Dawson that he had made a preacher of himself and lived in California. Whatever he did, I doubt seriously that he ever messed around with a married woman again.

CHAPTER 43

THAT'S ONE.......

Glenn Earl Jones had a nice flat land farm down in the Tradewater river bottoms near Shy Flat. Glenn Earl was a good ole boy and one of the original male chauvinists. He was a number one boss man. He waited till he was past thirty before he got hitched. But the Sizemore family moved into the She Flat area about the time Glenn Earl turned thirty six and it wasn't long before he was courting their old maid daughter - Sula Mae

And it wasn't long after they started courting that Sula Mae set her tender trap and captured Glenn Earl and announcements went out announcing the upcoming marriage of Glenn Earl and Sula Mae. The wedding was to be held at the Shy Flat Hardshell Baptist Church - public invited.

On the appointed day, Glenn Earl showed up in a freshly painted buggy pulled by a freshly curried and shod big bay horse. He got out, tied the horse to a tree and went into the church. A big crowd had turned out for the wedding and mainly the reception that would follow.

The reception was to be at the Sizemore Farm - just down the road. Mrs. Sizemore was Glenn Earl's sister and she had spread the word about all the food and drink she had fixed and bought for the event. Everyone knew that Glenn

Earl had money and was a free spender - and the word was that he had been to Mannington and bought a whole gallon of gin to "spike" the punch.

Anyway, as soon as the "I Do's" were said and the pronouncement made, Glenn Earl and Suly Mae headed for the buggy in a rainstorm of rice. Glenn Earl lifted her up and placed her in the buggy seat. He untied the horse and climbed in beside her, lifted the reins and whacked the horse on the rump and said "Giddy up hoss". The horse wouldn't giddy - it just stood there.

Glenn Earl didn't want to cause a commotion among the crowd which was watching. So Glenn Earl picked up the buggy whip and said "that's one" before he switched him with all his might. The horse jumped and started pulling the buggy and newlyweds down the road toward the Sizemore's.

Everything was proceeding nicely and they had kissed a time or two until they came to the old wooden bridge over the Tradewater River. The horse balked and would not cross the old wooden bridge. Glenn Earl ranted and raved and whipped the horse's rump but he refused to move.

Glenn Earl climbed out of the buggy and pried a 2x6 board loose from the old bridge and got back into the buggy. He stood up holding the board over his head and shouted "That's two" as he brought the board down hard right between the horse's ears. Clump! Clump! Clump! The horse moved forward across the bridge - staggering some but remaining on its feet.

Sula Mae said "Glenn Early honey - what is the matter with your horse? He seems like such a sweet and gentle animal." Glenn Earl replied "His just being honoree but I ain't going to put up with him much more."

But, sure enough - when they got to the drive to the Sizemore place - the horse refused to turn off the road - he balked again. Glenn Earl started cussing him again and got plumb livid in the face as he reached under the buggy seat and brought out an old pistol. He climbed down and went to the front of the horse, looked him in the eye, and said "That's three" - then POW! - right between the eyes.

Glenn Earl got back to the buggy and said "Honey climb down and we can walk from here."

Sula Mae really lit into him "I'll swear Glenn Earl Jones, you are the cruelest, meanest, and most insensitive man that I ever saw or heard tell of. Why did you shoot that poor animal?"

Glenn Earl stood there, looked her square in the eye, and said "That's one."

CHAPTER 44

FOOLED HER

The Ezell Adamases were hard shelled Baptists and never missed a Sunday at the French Lick Missionary Baptist Church.   There was a big blow up in the congregation over a sermon old Brother Raines had given about "Thou Shalt Not ......Fornicate." The end result was - Brother Raines was fired and a new minister - Brother Tate was brought in to replace him.

That first Sunday that Brother Tate preached, the Adamses invited him to come by their place for a country fried chicken dinner. He accepted of course.

Ezell had a problem. His Jersey cow was in heat and he had borrowed Delbert Turner's bull to "service" her. Delbert brought his bull by just as they were getting home from church.

Ezell called his 10 year old son, Joe Bob, outside and told him to stand by the gate and watch the bull and come tell him as soon as the bull took care of his "business" with the Jersey cow. In addition to the bull and the Jersey, there was an old black cow in the same pasture.

They had all sat down to the fried chicken dinner and were grilling the new pastor purty good when Joe Bob came running in and yelled "Pa, that bull just screwed the old black cow." The preacher asked "What are you talking about son? Ezell got up and said "Preacher, you will have to excuse the boy - he made a mistake." He led Joe Bob outside and scolded him and told him to go watch some more. Joe Bob asked, "But what am I supposed to say next time?" Ezell thought a minute and said "You say - The Bull <u>fooled</u> the Jersey." Joe Bob went back to his assignment and Ezell went back to his plate of chicken. Before he cleaned his plate, Joe Bob popped in the door again and announced "The Bull fooled the Jersey."

Ezelle said "That's good - thank you Son." Joe Bob reared back and in a much louder voice said "Yeah, he really fooled that Jersey cow good - he screwed the old black cow again."

CHAPTER 45

PINCH AND JUDY

Pinch Wilson was such a tightwad that he had squeezed the crap of every buffalo nickel - if you ever got a nickel with a skinny buffalo on it you - can bet it was one that Pinch had a holt of. Judy Fox was almost as tight (or so they say). It seems they were meant for one another.

When they were both in their mid twenties they met at a Holy Roller tent meeting in Nebo. (It didn't cost nothing to go to a tent meeting - and they could be right entertaining at times). Anyway, Pinch took a shine to Judy and before long they were courting - right steady. More often than not they went to Church socials, etc. that was free. Maybe once every week or so, Pinch would spend 30 cents and take Judy to the picture show.

It didn't seem like they were getting along too good though - they were forever arguing and yelling at one another. But they must have been - one weekend they eloped and went somewhere down near Knoxville, Tennessee and got married.

Pinch had a good job at the mines and rumor had it that he had a purty good size bank account at the Citizens State Bank. I know for a fact that he owned one of the newest and best Ford V8 pickup trucks in Charleston. They rented a house from Phillip Boynton and set up housekeeping. In less than seven months Judy had a baby - a little girl. (Some said pre-mature - but others said not - you know how folks gossip). After the baby was born the arguing re-commenced.

I delivered some groceries to their next door neighbors, The Hudson's, about a month after the birthing. Mrs. Hudson made me sit down and drink coffee and eat a donut and tell her the Dawson gossip before I left. Mr. Hudson joined us. After I ran out of stuff to talk about, Mrs. Hudson started talking about the neighbors, especially Pinch and Judy and the premature baby. She said they were back to fighting life cats and dogs. She said they fought all the time - she didn't see how their marriage would last. Mr. Hudson chirped up "She looks like she's pregnant again so they must be getting along sometimes." And I recon he was right - Judy had a young un about every 10 months for the next five years.

The boys at the mines said all Pinch ever wanted to talk about was women and sex. Some said he was a sex fanatic. Old Jake Eli said if he didn't stop using his little head instead of his big head he was going to get into more trouble than he could handle. Ron Smith arguing "Naw, he's got enough money stashed away that he can hire one of them high priced lawyers in Madisonville and get away with anything." Jake asked "How much money you think Pinch has put away?" And Ron responded "I don't know exactly but I've heard he's got enough that he could stack it and climb up on it and see clear to Kuttawa."

Time proved one of them right. Within a year Judy caught Pinch humping the cleaning lady in their back bedroom one day and filed for divorce. Pinch contested it - knowing it was going to cost him a bunch of money. He pleaded with Judy to drop the filing but she wouldn't do it. The case came to trial and the old judge was listing to the arguments about custody of the children. (He had already decided to grant the divorce). It was Judy's turn and she said "Judge, all them babies came from my womb, they grew inside me, and they should always be mine." The old judge looked at Pinch and said "That's a strong argument - what do you say?" Pinch thought for a long time and finally said "Judge, if I put a nickel in one of them vending machines and a RC Cola come out of it - who would that RC belong to - me or that machine?"

We don't know how he done it but Pinch finally got Judy to back down and let him move back in. Later, Ron Smith just come right out and asked him. Pinch said "I offered her a big diamond ring or a Packard car if she would take me back." Ron said "You got her the Packard - right?" "Naw, - the ring" responded Pinch. Ron said "Man, you're crazy - you can't wear that ring but think how nice it would be - driving around in that big Packard automobile. Why in heck did you get her a ring? Pinch said "Ever look for fake Packard car?

Pinch never mended his ways and they continued to fight like cats and dogs - even old cats and dogs. Finally, it caught up with Pinch. Old Rufus Barnes caught Pinch in bed with his wife and blew his brains out with a twelve gauge shotgun. The undertaker took his body to his shop and contacted Judy about burying him. Judy, who by now had heard the details of his death and was extremely angry and upset, said "Just dig a hole and throw the sorry S.O.B. in it - and send me the bill. I'll pay it if it ain't over $50.

The next day the owner of the local newspaper stopped by their house and asked how he should word the obituary. Judy said - just put <u>Pinch</u> <u>Died</u>. The newspaper man said - you can't just say Pinch died - you should put a lot more in an obituary - it's only 10 cents a word. Judy wouldn't change - she said "Pinch Died - and that's it." The newspaper man said - there is a <u>five</u> word minimum! Judy thought for a minute and said, "Let's start over....... Pinch died. Pickup for sale."

CHAPTER 46

BEAUTIFUL DREAMER

The railroad track cut across the back forty acres of Bob Dunbar's farm -- about a half mile from the Claxton Hill. In the still of a summer night while sitting on the front porch of the Dunbar's house, you could hear the lonesome whistle of the freight trains coming out of Dawson with a load of coal and trying to gather up a head of steam so they could make the grade over the Claxton Hill. Before the train cleared the hill, it would be slowed to about a walk. The next place where the train would slow down or, maybe, stop was Princeton--about 15 miles west of there.

Many a times folk in those parts hopped aboard a train when it was climbing the Claxton grade and rode it to Princeton. Beings as how it was so handy to Dunbar's--he rode it quite regularly, in fact so regular that he came to dream about it often. The dream was always the same--about a beautiful redheaded woman in Princeton.

Bob was a happily married man (if there is any such animal); and he never told anybody (especially his wife) except Shorty Morton--his best friend bout his dream.

Bob and Shorty had grown up together and been lifelong friends--true friends. They had been through the thick and the thin together, and their friendship was bonded by many experiences which they had shared over the years--some secretive.

In the summer-time Shorty, who never married, would walk up to the Dunbar's place after he took care of the milking , and other chores around his farm and sit on the front porch with Bob and his wife, Edna. They would sit and talk for an hour or so; and Edna would always be the first to leave --generally with the excuse that she wanted to go finish the quilt which she was working on. (Really, she would go into the house and fix herself a "snack," eat, and look at the Sears Roebuck catalog. She weighed about 170

pounds and stood about 5 feet 5 inches in her' bare feet. (She wasn't exactly your sex symbol.)

After Edna would leave, the boys would sit in silence for awhile; but, directly, one or the other would break the silence and before long they would talking "man talk." Just before Shorty would start to leave, Bob always told him about the dream he had the night before.

"Shorty," he would say, "last night I had the bestest dream. I drempt that Edna wanted some candy and stuff late yesterday so I decided to take a little trip over to Princeton to see what was goin' on and to get the candy for her. I shaved, took a bath, put on my Sunday best, and walked back to the track and hopped a freight to Princeton about sundown. Well, I got to Princeton, went downtown and messed around for awhile, and then went over to the Rexall Drug Store to buy the candy and stuff.

"The lady who waited on me was the purtiest redheaded female you ever want to lay eyes on. Well, you know me--I struck up a friendly conversation with her and afore long we were hittin it off real good. It turns out that she's a grass widow and lives by herself there in Princeton. I had me a root beer and kind of hung around the drug store 'til they commenced to shut 'er down. (I already was beginning to get ideas, you see.)

"Anyway, I waited outside the store while they shut 'off the lights and closed the store; and this redhead came out, followed by old Tightwad Woodburn --the feller who runs the store. I asked Ruby (that was her name) if I could walk her home. Old Woodburn. really give me the "go to heck" looks; but I didn't pay him no mind--especially when Ruby said, "Why yes, Bob, I would enjoy your company."

"She told me as we were walking down the street that old Woodburn drove her home in his T-Model every night; and, on several occasions, had tried to get an invite into her house; but she always refused his "advances." We carried on a pleasant conversation and in no time were in front of her house. I says, "Ruby, I think by now that you know that I've got the same 'idea that old Woodburn has had--are you going to turn me away too?" "Wal, she looked into these blue eyes of mine a full minute before answering, "Come on in, Bob, You've given me the same idea and it has been a long time since I've had a man's company" I nearly messed in my pants when she said that--but I didn't. Instead, I could feel my emotions starting to stiffen up and I followed her into the house. You can imagine the rest of my dream--that was the best I ever had."

By now Shorty was all sexed up and he would have to head back to his farm and old Minnie. And I suppose that the telling of this beautiful dream had Bob "sexed up" enough to go in and hop in the bed with fat Edna. Whatever--the dream continued for months and months; and Bob kept telling the dream over and over to Shorty--night after night. Some of the details would change back and forth with each telling but the basics remained the same--trip to Princeton-- beautiful redhead--mating.

Finally, after hearing this dream repeated about the humpteenth time, Shorty announced one night that he too had dreamt the night before. Bob said, "Shorty, that's wonderful, tell me about it."

Shorty said, "Shucks, I can't tell 'em like you can, Bob." Bob kept eggin' him on and finally Shorty began.

"Last night, just as I was finishing up chores and getting ready to walk up here to your place for a visit I heard this motor car sputterin' up the road. When it got to my place, it pulled in and stopped. I went outside to see who it was and it turned out to be these two beautiful women who were lost. They were with the

Bisbee carnival and were looking for Saint Charles--some prank in Dawson had sent them out the wrong road.

"They was both right buxomy, blond-headed, blue-eyed, about twenty-five or twenty-six and were sisters from Mississippi. They had this juggling and sword-swallowing act in the carnival which they demonstrated for me.

Anyway, it was late and they was lost so I offered them supper--which they accepted immediately--and after giving them fair warning that I was a bachelor, I offered to let them sleep at my place. They looked at one another and giggled and said to me, "Charley, you're sure nice to us and so cute--we'll make it up to you in bed. But, it would be even nicer if you had a friend to come over and help you."

By now, Bob had really gotten involved in the story (the same as Shorty did every time he heard about the gorgeous redhead in Princeton) and excitedly he yelled at Charlie, "Why, you little rascal--why didn't you come over and get me?"

Shorty meekly replied, "I did, Bob, but Edna said you had just hopped on the freight train for Princeton."

- THE END -

That's all Folks - now go buy another of my books.

BOOKS WRITTEN BY
BILL R. THOMAS

Title	Brief Description
1) A Summer on Piney Creek	A Summer Spent with Friend Living in a Cave on Piney Creek (Kentucky)
2) Hickory Fired Tobacco, Moonshine Whiskey, Beautiful Horses, and Fast Women	Kentucky Based Short Stories
3) Bill T's Texas Bob Tales	Texas Based Short Stories
4) I Smell Smoke	Authors Experience as B-47 Crew Member in Strategic Air Command
5) My Most Memorable Adventures - One Hunting and One Fishing	Hunting Trip in Mexico and Fishing Trip in Alaska
6) The Accumulated Wisdom of the Bugscuffle Domino, Whittle and Spit Club	Philosophy and Wisdom Gained Over a Colorful Lifetime
7) The T-Bone Ranch	Developing a Cattle Ranch in Montague County, Texas
8) A Wild Shot In The Dark	Autobiography - Birth Through Air Force
9) The Debits Are On The Left, The Credits Are By The Window	Autobiography - Air Force to Present

www.ingramcontent.com/pod-product-compliance
Lightning Source LLC
La Vergne TN
LVHW011226080426
835509LV00005B/345